The ArtScroll Series®

Rabbi Nosson Scherman / Rabbi Meir Zlotowitz

*General Editors*

# All Things

Published by

Mesorah Publications, ltd

# Considered...

## From a woman's point of view...

*by Yaffa Ganz*

FIRST EDITION
First Impression . . . October 1990


Published and Distributed by
**MESORAH PUBLICATIONS, Ltd.**
Brooklyn, New York 11232

Distributed in Israel by
MESORAH MAFITZIM / J. GROSSMAN
Rechov Harav Uziel 117
Jerusalem, Israel

Distributed in Europe by
J. LEHMANN HEBREW BOOKSELLERS
20 Cambridge Terrace
Gateshead, Tyne and Wear
England NE8 1RP

Distributed in Australia & New Zealand by
GOLD'S BOOK & GIFT CO.
36 William Street
Balaclava 3183, Vic., Australia

Distributed in South Africa by
KOLLEL BOOKSHOP
22 Muller Street
Yeoville 2198
Johannesburg, South Africa

Typography by CompuScribe at ArtScroll Studios, Ltd.
4401 Second Avenue / Brooklyn, N.Y. 11232 / (718) 921-9000

Printed in the United States of America by Noble Book Press Corp.
Bound by Sefercraft Quality Bookbinders, Ltd., Brooklyn, N.Y.

This book is dedicated
to those who kindle the Shabbos candles
and keep the light of Torah aglow.
To all of the wonderful Jewish women
I have been privileged to meet
and know and love and learn from.
And especially to the memory of my mother
Dorothy Devorah Siegel z"l
who always held her candle high.

# Foreword

ALL THINGS CONSIDERED, it's a pretty good world out there. The trouble is that we don't have much time to think about it. There's so much to keep up with, to watch out for, and to take care of, that we can barely catch our breath between one thing and the next.

But if, as our Sages say, the mind is the seat of the soul, then our thoughts are more than mere electronic impulses flitting around our brains, haphazardly seeking solutions to our many problems. Like some magnificent, custom-designed ship of the spirit, the mind creates and houses the thoughts which help us navigate through the sea of life. When we fail to set a course and utilize this powerful, G-d- given vessel, we are swept passively along in strong currents not of our making, unthinkingly doing the things everyone else is doing without ever stopping to ask why, what for, or at what price.

But even when we do stop, look around, and attempt to get our bearings, we soon discover that not everyone perceives things in the same light. Women in particular tend to see things differently than men. Their view of life is the result of a singular blend of mind, matter, heart and soul, and expression perhaps, of the *bina yeseira* — the additional dimension of wisdom — with which they were blessed.

Because of their unique perceptions and responses, one well-placed feminine critique can have greater impact than reams of reasons to the contrary. As G-d said to Abraham long ago, "... all that Sarah says to you, hearken to her voice." And in an aggressive, unstable world, a woman's sensitive, subtle approach can provide safety and respite — a quiet, comfortable corner to rest in before returning to the fray.

*Sometimes,* the best way to keep our perspective in today's hectic society is simply to laugh. Women are good at that, too. Blessed as they are with the life-sustaining gifts of loving and nurturing, even their humor contains a particularly wholesome and healing quality.

Contemplating the ever-changing contemporary scene through a woman's eye opens new vistas and makes new insights possible. And while every woman has her own individual ship of the spirit to sail, her own course to follow, her own domain to survey, many of our experiences and observations are shared ones. All things considered, the view from our side of the deck is definitely intriguing.

## Acknowledgments

Our rabbis teach us that we are obligated to give thanks where thanks are due. To be ungrateful is to be remiss and to depart from the way of G-d.

And so I give thanks, firstly, to He who gave me whatever talents I may possess for putting thoughts and feelings into words; and secondly, for the opportunities He has sent my way to get the words into print.

To Rabbi Nosson Scherman for his goodwill, humor and common sense. Writing in a light and humorous matter on matters of serious import can be a difficult occupation. He helped the "shidduch" along and made the road smoother.

To Shmuel Blitz of ArtScroll Jerusalem, publisher and friend, who refused to ever be pessimistic.

To my sister Beverly who read, and read, and reread.

And most of all, to my husband who, in his non-existent "spare" time, read, edited, encouraged, suggested, supported and served as my personal Talmudic, halachic, historical and general encyclopedia. His erudition saved me untold time and effort, and his warm, wonderful humor added countless plums to the pudding.

Yaffa Ganz
Jerusalem

# Table of Contents

## There's No Place Like Home: Life in Israel

## Soulscan: A Jewish Point of View

## Just Passing Through: Memory Lane

## Glossary

# All Things
## Considered...

# It's a Woman's World

*Although they are usually referred to as the "weaker sex," women possess unusual strengths. There is no lack of stories about great men, of course, but the sneaking suspicion remains: Women are the world's real Rock of Gibraltar. Ponder the following true story.*

*A Jewish woman from a small shtetl near Pinsk decided that the time had come to follow her husband to America. She packed the bedding, the pots and pans, the clothing, her brass candlesticks, and sacks of toasted black bread, enough for a two-month journey. When all was ready, she gathered up her* pecklach *and her ten children and began her trek to the goldineh medineh.*

*I shall not burden you with all the traumatic details of that journey except to say that it turned out to be a five-month nightmare, enough to make anyone's hair stand on end. Her supply of bread ran out; her passports were taken away; her money was stolen; she was turned off the trains, stranded at borders, and missed the boat. Eventually, somehow, she arrived in America with herself and her children reasonably intact. She was still sane too. Granted that this was a woman of unusual fortitude. Nonetheless, I think that even most men will agree, this was a woman's act par excellence.*

❦ ❦ ❦

*But women are more than just strong. They are smart and loving, sympathetic and joyful and creative. They are endowed with certain instinctive gifts whose exact definition has eluded scientific analysis to this day: the* binah yeseirah *(extra understanding) which our Sages mentioned a few thousand years ago, and the special* neshamah *which G-d crafted for them to function as the* ezer, *that indispensable partner to man.*

*As part of their unique equipment, women have special "antennae" which run like long threads throughout human history and society, keeping them finely attuned to the needs of the people they know and love. The information they supply helps make our world a happier, better, and more Heavenly place.*

*Perhaps this is why the* Maharal *of Prague views women as being a higher form of creation; a creature whose innate spiritual make-up is somehow more in tune with the world of the spirit, therefore requiring the performance of fewer* mitzvos *than men in order to achieve spiritual perfection.*

*One thing is certain. The world of women is rich and varied; usually complicated and challenging; often hectic. And always rewarding.*

# Utterly Unique

ead, heart and imagination — these are qualities shared by all human beings, but when they appear in women, either singly or in marvelous combinations, they take on added dimensions and produce utterly unique results. For example:

Born in Lithuania to a family of *talmidei chachamim*, Mrs. S. is definitely a Woman of the Mind. As the eldest child in the house, she had been given a thorough Jewish education, not only in *limudei kodesh,* but in things like Hebrew grammar and Jewish history as well. She knew how to read and write Yiddish and Hebrew, of course, and also Lithuanian, Polish and some Russian.

She was sixteen when her father, a far-seeing man, sent her away at the outbreak of World War II. It was the last time she ever saw her family.

She made her way alone, across Poland and Russia, hoping to reach England. Keeping her wits about her, she found ways of keeping safe as she moved across a blazing continent. She wound up unexpectedly, as did many others, in Shanghai where she met and married a young yeshivah man.

Her husband's untimely death a few years later found her in New York with five small children. Forced to earn her own living, she entered the world of *chinuch.* She taught, raised her children, persevered and, *baruch Hashem,* prevailed.

Today, many years later, Mrs. S. is the matriarch of a large and highly respected clan which boasts three generations of Torah scholars and outstanding women. She herself now lives in Jerusalem where, despite her cosmopolitan Lithuanian background, she teaches in a very chassidishe, Yiddish-speaking girls' school. They love her.

Like many of her contemporaries from the pre-World War II Lithuanian community, her expansive knowledge, her broad education, her sophistication have all served her — and the Jewish community — well. These Lithuanian women shared a Jewish educational ethos which barely exists today, but which we might well emulate.

※　※　※

Another "brainy" female on the scene is an American *chassidishe rebbetzin* from a prestigious family. Despite the difference in outlook and background, she is amazingly similar to Mrs. S. The depth and breadth of her education is something to think about. A Bais Yaakov graduate, teacher, social worker, possessor of an advanced degree, mother of many children, bubby of many more, and great-grandmother of a growing few, she is a woman who could rejuvenate the Jewish people on a desert island. This is a woman who thinks. If they put her in the Pentagon, or on some National Planning Committee, I have no doubt she would tidy up all national problems in no time at all. But then again, so could her mother. Or her sisters. Even her cousins aren't bad. Theirs is a superb collection of brainy, *chessed*-filled, feminine genes, second to none!

❅ ❅ ❅

Nominations for Women of the Heart are many, but I have two favorites. The first is Esther, a young Hungarian woman brought to the United States by relatives after World War II. She spent several debilitating years in the camps, married, and gave birth to two children. Upon her arrival in America, it was discovered that she had leukemia. At that time, the disease was always fatal.

She was granted an additional ten or fifteen years of life which were spent alternately either in hospitals or in hospitality, opening her apartment (she had never moved up enough to afford a house) to those less fortunate than she. And these being the years after the war, there were many.

You could never enter Esther's house without finding a few new faces. It was a Hungarian-Yiddish-speaking outpost; her boarders weren't the kind who had learned English yet. She put them on the sofa, on the floors, and gave the married couples her bedroom. She fed them and lent them money and found them jobs. She put their kids in school and made her own children responsible for them. She encouraged them and laughed and cried with them and loved them. She went broke several times taking care of them. Small in stature, she was a phenomenally big woman with a warm, wide smile, even when she was thin and emaciated from her illness.

Neither famous nor well known outside of her own circle of unfortunates, she surely received a royal welcome when she put in her appearance at the Heavenly Court. She left behind a legacy filled with *zechuyos* for her children, who are very much like her.

❅ ❅ ❅

Mrs. O. is another Woman of the Heart. Not that her brains aren't in wonderful working order; they are. But whenever I think of her, I see lines of the thousands of people she has fed, clothed and supported throughout her life. I always wondered, where does she find them — all these people who are really poor? Really hungry? Our *tzedakah* always seemed to go to schools or institutions, but to really, truly poor people? We didn't usually see them. Yet they were there, and she found them. Or perhaps they found her.

When her family moved to Israel, Mrs. O. was out organizing her new constituency even before her household was unpacked — quietly, with no fanfare, no funds, no organization behind her. She used her telephone, took buses, *shlepped* packages, and did what had to be done. Even now, when she is no longer physically able to do what she did for so long, her phone continues to ring and the requests continue to pour in.

Mrs. O. is the kind of lady who takes the neighbor's impossible, screaming child out for a walk because the mother is at her wits' end. She is the kind who cries when confronted with human suffering such as a fire which killed several black children in a slum building many years ago.

"Why was she crying?" someone asked. Did she know any of those children? "Do I have to know them personally to cry?" she asked. "A child is a child, whether you know him or not. And a human tragedy is a sorrow for all human beings."

I was only a girl when I heard that conversation, but it has remained with me. When we limit human sympathy, we limit our own humanity.

🦋 🦋 🦋

And then there are the Creative Souls. I've come across many, but two jewels stand out. Both young, highly individualistic, and marvelously gifted, they leave me feeling as though I am all thumbs.

The first walked a long, lonely, arduous path until she

reached her present place on our planet. Yet she has retained an exquisite sense of humor and a healthy measure of joy. Hers is a soul full of music which finds its expression in poetry, drama, dance and song. A gold mine of the spirit, she finds countless ways to express the beauty of G-d's world, and with her own manifold gifts, she enriches the world of those around her.

My second star has a direct line from heaven to her hands. Whether it's painting, drawing, sewing, knitting, embroidering; sculpturing, woodworking or making shoes — if it's something you do with your hands, she does it. And what creations she turns out! Joyous things, full of light and balance and harmony. Pictures and paintings which lift up the soul and help you understand that G-d has given some tiny, infinitesimal piece of His Divine Creativity to Man — or in this case, to Woman. And if one woman, using her mind and her hands, can create such wonderful things, imagine what the Creator of the Universe can do!

Come to think of it, He has done unimaginably wonderful things already. And He has created Man, culminating in that ultimate, utterly unique creature called Woman.

# Let's Do It My Way

"Thank you very much, but I really don't think that color blouse will do. I know the colors are almost identical, but the shade I'm looking for is slightly different."

"No thanks, I don't need a new can-opener. I know they're the hottest thing on the market, but I don't need one anyway."

"I'm sorry, but I really cannot host three additional kids this Shabbos. I am already taking four."

"Yes, I know the meeting has to be somewhere, but I'm afraid it just can't be at my house. The last two meetings were here, remember?"

"I'll bet you a banana split that not every one of your friends is going, but even if they are, you still can't go. Because I said so, that's why."

"I need the telephone now. I know you're doing your homework on the phone with Judy. No, I will not accept responsibility if you fail the exam tomorrow."

"I'd really rather not discuss it. It's her business, not ours."

"It's just too bad if absolutely everyone at the wedding will be wearing a new dress. I only wore this one once and it's beautiful and I happen to like it. I will look lovely. It does not look worn out!"

❁   ❁   ❁

If any of the above are responses you wish you could make but seldom do, then you are in need of some help. A little encouragement. Some good old J.A.T. (Jewish Assertiveness Training).

Assertiveness Training is in style nowadays. If exercised with care, it can be a good thing, but only if we remember that: (1) assertiveness is strong stuff. Like pepper, a little bit goes a long way; and (2) while doing your own thing, your own way, it's always wise to do it gently. Today's "Doing Your Own Thing" is often just a cover up for plain, old-fashioned, selfish egotism. And when expressed assertively, it usually means "I'm going to do exactly what I want, no matter what. So you'd better get out of my way!" which is not exactly the Jewish way.

The Jewish Way often requires its followers to lay aside their own wishes, plans, desires and ambitions, and to do something else first. Something specific, like a *mitzvah*. Something which turns our attention towards *Hashem*, rather than towards ourselves. Something which looks to another person's needs, rather than to our own.

Women are particularly adept at thinking of other people first, but instead of patting us on the back for a job well done, contemporary culture frowns upon our "lack of independence." I was therefore particularly pleased when I came across the following paragraph by a popular, best-selling authoress: ". . . female dependence appears to be less a wish to be protected than a wish to be part of a web of human relationships; a wish not only to get, but to give, loving care. . . It also means, however, that identity, for women, has more to do with intimacy than with separateness."

❧ ❧ ❧

Yes it does. We are the ones who are charged with keeping things — and people — together, not separate. We are usually more sensitive, more communicative, and more dependent on human connections than the male half of the species. And there's good reason G-d made us this way.

Nonetheless, each of us has her own special "way," her own private garden to care for; and if we fail to do so, the loss is more than personal. It's a public, environmental loss, affecting and impoverishing everyone around us.

Yet not only do women's personal vineyards often go untended, but many of us even forget we have one! We also forget that just like everyone else, we too are entitled to say, "No," or "Enough," or "I Want," or "I Will." Even a simple "No, thank you" can become difficult and guilt-ridden when most of one's time is spent saying "Yes, of course I will."

But if we don't have our say and do our thing, how will the world learn that Sara plays the piano so beautifully, and that Tova arranges silk flowers? That Chani loves to draw and that Meira is a whiz at balancing checkbooks and doing crossword puzzles? And who would have thought that mindless Lizzie is a computer programmer, and that helpless, little Miriam is a lifeguard, and that Anita (whose home is absolutely spotless) does ceramics in her basement where she looks like a messy cement mixer, while Lily (whose housekeeping is very casual, to put it mildly) runs a precise, highly-organized business from her den? And did you know that Barbara is a marvelous photographer?

Each of these very different women shares a highly

developed sense of self, despite the fact that most of their days are taken up with caring for, worrying about, developing, protecting, and seeing to someone else. They each know that they are precious and distinct, if somewhat domestically burdened on a day-to-day basis. Tolstoy, in *War and Peace,* spoke about the "endless multiplicity of men's minds." He might have mentioned "women's" too!

*Chazal* taught us long ago that each person is a world unto himself, possessing, as he or she does, a unique and irreplaceable soul. Each person's life is something that has no possible substitute or exchange, which means that nothing and no one can take *your* place.

Just think of the *mitzvah* of *"v'ahavta lereyacha kamocha"* — you shall love your neighbor as you love yourself. We are commanded to love others. How much? As much as we love ourselves! But if our own self-love and self-esteem is faulty, it is difficult to relate to the next person in a positive manner. It might be summed up in the vernacular with the name of the once-popular book *I'm OK, You're OK. I'm OK* has to come first.

It's definitely something to think about the next time you are feeling low on the totem pole.

# Forty Plus is Fine With Me

have discovered that with the passing of years — at least forty of them — the women I know have all become much wiser. Of course I can't prove it, but nonetheless, I'm sure it's true. After all, having spent so much time in this world, one can be fairly certain that one has learnt something. Think of all the places we've been, the people we've met, the difficult situations we've had to deal with, and here we are — still fairly intact, functioning (usually), competent (more or less), and even smiling (most of the time). All things considered, that's nothing to sneeze at.

We have learned that life's unending chain of daily emergencies and catastrophes usually get straightened out. We know that although we are not able to solve every dilemma, someone else may come up with a bright idea. Or, if left alone for a while, a problem might just solve itself. And most important of all, we have learned that some problems are not solvable, so there is no use knocking yourself out trying. They simply have to be lived with and somehow accommodated. If you're patient enough, they may dissolve or disappear unaided.

For example, a mere twenty-five years ago, in ancient, far-away, pre-Pamper, no-dryer days, I thought that one of life's most taxing problems was five or six consecutive days of Israeli rain, with no way to dry the diapers. As one wet day followed another, my nerves, constantly damp and chilly, approached a state of total disintegration.

Yet even then, in those primitive times, the diapers dried. Strung across our tiny living room in a two-by-four house in a small settlement in the northern Negev, they looked like ghostly white tobacco leaves hung out in front of a kerosene, sun-like stove. We changed and turned them by the hour, sometimes finding them browned, as well as dried (tobacco leaves, anyone?). The point is, we managed, albeit with some degree of difficulty, in a situation I then considered well-nigh impossible. And then the sun came out. It usually does, if only you're patient enough.

Nowadays, when I'm twenty-five years smarter, a problem like wet diapers would no longer daunt me. At most, I would consider it a pain in the neck, find some solution, and get on with the business of living.

Aside from putting problems in their proper perspective, when you are carrying around forty-years-plus-some on your shoulders, the added weight serves as a ballast, keeping you sensibly anchored to the ground. This may slow you down a bit or make you seem less adventuresome to the younger crowd, but it also heightens your appreciation for life, because by now you better understand how precious each day is.

For time, that transient material of which the fabric of our lives is woven, is given to us piece by piece, one minute, one hour, one day at a time, and then that moment is gone forever. So with our forty-plus wisdom, we tend to be more thoughtful of how we fill our days and weave our cloth. Or at least, we try to be.

I will admit that there are less pleasant aspects to being over forty, such as looking in the mirror. Your head may be covered, but those gray hairs under your wig are still an unpleasant surprise. And those little lines around your mouth and eyes — where did they ever come from? And you aren't fat (Heaven forbid!), but still, your wedding gown was three sizes smaller. And worst of all, when you go shopping, the really chic clothes don't quite seem to fit. Or is it true what everyone (everyone your age, that is) is saying, that nowadays, they are simply making clothes smaller and smaller? (How else can you explain the explosion of large size shops across the U.S.? Not everyone can be gaining weight!)

*Baruch Hashem* for the laws of *tznius!* It takes a bit of living (like forty years' worth) to fully appreciate their inherent wisdom. Aside from their other functions, they do much to save the psyche from the ravages of age and to help us preserve a positive self-image. And after forty, preservation is an important word.

We know that a few extra wrinkles or pounds are not a measure of our value. True, we do apply the creams and cosmetics, but with a healthy dose of humor and, with all due respect to the cosmetics industry, not a little skepticism as to their efficacy!

There are other minor annoyances to being over forty, such as teen-age daughters who make quick mental calculations and discover that their mothers are nearing a state of antiquity. It's hard on everyone's ego, I admit. But if a girl is fourteen, what does she expect her mother to be ... twenty-five? Especially when she has a twenty-six year old brother in the house!

Despite these minor setbacks, we mature women get over the initial bumps and settle down. As the old Yiddish saying goes — you have just two choices in life: either you get older . . . or you don't.

Not only are women getting older, they are liking it, too, for age brings freedoms, first of which is freedom from many of your own long-harbored *meshugasim.* For by this stage in life, most of us have managed to rid ourselves of all sorts of unrealistic demands and expectations, such as three perfectly cooked, well-balanced, beautifully arranged meals on the table every day.

I, for example, have fed thousands of people in my life and set some pretty fancy tables, as tables go, but I have yet to manage a "dinner party" á la Good Housekeeping. It took me a while to understand that I'm not made to preside in perfect splendor like a movie star amidst tinkling glasses of champagne and hors d'oeuvres. It's not my style — and it's surely not my husband's — and now that I've finally made peace with that fact, I'm thoroughly relieved.

By the age of forty, we have learned how to say "no" to many things we should have said "no" to years ago. But a lack of self-confidence got in the way, causing us much wasted time and annoyance. And to top it off, with most of us, our hard-earned self-confidence is nicely tempered by a measure of self-knowledge.

For at this point in our lives, we more or less know what to expect of ourselves, where our weaknesses lie and when they might interrupt us uninvitedly. And, better yet, our family and friends know them too, thereby making them more tolerant of us, and us of them, in what is surely a respectable, harmonious, two-way street.

Last, and perhaps most lovely of all, is the freedom of time. There is not less to do when you are over forty, but you are freer to do new and different things. The exhilarating but physically exhausting days of raising very young children are usually over. Your nights are your own, to twist and turn, or to sleep soundly, but at your own speed. (Babies are always wonderful, but they seem less so at three in the morning.) I think the general rule of thumb could be summed up as: The further you get from forty, the harder it is to get up at night. Which, of course, is what makes grandchildren such a pleasure. They are yours for enjoying, not raising; crystallized pleasure, without the doctors and the diapers.

And luxury of all luxuries, if one day you don't feel like doing much of anything, you can sit yourself down and do just that.

All in all, it's not a bad world. As the doors from the kitchen and the laundry open up a bit, things look interestingly wide out there. The only drawback is, that as the kids grow up and out, they come crowding back in with a new generation in tow. And even though we are a young forty-plus, we still become, *baruch Hashem*, bubbies, and as such, we are handed a new package of responsibilities. Normally, these entail extensive kitchen duties, especially on *Shabbos* and holidays. And the larger the new generation becomes, the larger these responsibilities loom. You can always tell your own child that you have no time to bake today, but how can you tell a grandchild that bubby has no cookies in the house?

But whether one goes in for cooking, culture, cosmetics or computers, having come so far and accomplished so much, we will, please G-d, continue our journey gracefully — smiling, thankful, and young at heart.

# The Gift of Speech

ur Sages tell us that of the ten measures of speech granted to human beings, nine were granted to women. Men tend to view this in a rather uppity manner, as if woman's expanded word-ratio were some sort of defect. When told, however, that men possess greater mathematical abilities than women, they seem to feel that this is indicative of superior talents! One could argue that more math makes for chillier, more robotic minds, while more talk makes for warmer, more humane people, couldn't one?

Especially when you remember what Onkelos and Rashi say about the verse "And G-d formed Man . . . and Man became a living soul." All animals are "living souls," but Adam and Chavah were the greatest of all because they were granted the powers of understanding and speech. Now if speech elevates us to a higher spiritual level, then wouldn't you think that *more*

speech endows the recipient with *additional* greatness?

In any event, if this is the way G-d created females, rest assured there's a good reason for it. Instead of squirming uncomfortably about their tendency to talk, women should practice and promote it!

We have, for example, so much of importance to say. When women get together, in an astoundingly short period of time (and often in few words), vital information is passed on. How so and so is feeling; what brilliant pearls of wisdom her granddaughter produced; how the neighborhood *mikveh,* or committee, or supermarket is functioning; who needs which help with what; which vital activities are going on next week and the week after.

Men, on the other hand, have detailed discussions which can only be described as dull. Facts, figures, machines and politics are their piece of the pie. In all fairness, it must be mentioned that *bnei Torah* spend a good deal of their time "talking in learning," but the time that's left over is usually run-of-the-mill men-talk.

Take cars, for example. Car topics are a male favorite. Gears, motors, tires, and other related parts are items of intense interest. Women limit dry, practical subjects like these (if they bother to discuss them at all) to a sentence or two. What they zero in on is how helpful or annoying the man at the service station was. Whether or not he saved you the trouble of checking the oil. Whether he made you wait for your change. It's the human element which attracts their attention.

And it's precisely the human element which is the reason women were granted a "larger measure" of speech (a fact which, by the way, is physiologically based. Women have been scientifically — not just folkloristically — found to be more facile with language than men. It's all neatly programmed into their brain cells.) Physical contact and speech are the two most potent and primary forms of human communication, and if women, who are in charge of Primary Education for the human race, are not proficient in words and songs and hugs and kisses (and a slap or two when necessary), then who should be?

You see, there is so much for the average mother to say, sing, tell, instruct, repeat, report, and interrogate, that in order to do her job well, she must have more speech units at her disposal than the average man.

She uses them fairly well, too. At least among the people I know. Because of their facility with language, women can express kindness, compassion, love, and sympathy more easily than men. Men are surely just as kind, compassionate and loving as women, but women are more verbal about it. And since we can't very well expect the next person to read our minds or hearts, the ability to give expression to these thoughts and feelings is our own particular Divinely-bestowed gift. A "heart-to-heart talk" is very much a woman's affair.

This "gift" can be exploited or put to bad use, of course, as can any G-d-given quality. But bad-mouthing (no pun intended) women is unfair. Poor speech habits are evenly distributed between both halves of humanity, and *lashon hara* is a sexless sin. Attributing most of it to females is a gross distortion. Just remember, the Chafetz Chaim didn't write his book for women!

*Chazal* said that speech contains the power of life or death. Unlike a written word, a word once spoken cannot be erased. It is indelibly imprinted on the listener's mind. And since we never really know what is in the next person's mind or heart, we never really know what impact our words will have on him. Which is why we have to be so careful about what we say, for our speech can be a miraculous balm — or a potent weapon.

How many times do we say, "I could kick myself for having said that!" Things just slip out when we aren't thinking; we say them to be funny or witty or wise and we end up being sorry. Sometimes the damage we cause is to ourselves, which is probably better than causing it to someone else.

Of course possessing nine measures of speech has a few other drawbacks as well. When every woman has so much to say, it's sometimes difficult to find the time to listen to the next gal. Fortunately, our interest in hearing is at least as great as our interest in imparting, and so an amicable balance is usually achieved.

Generally speaking, people with a modicum of Jewish learning are more careful with their words, both the ones they speak and the ones they listen to. In contrast, I have often overheard conversations on buses, in waiting rooms, in hospitals, or on park benches where I am forever taken aback, not only at the topics of conversation, but at the lack of restraint. People discuss the most personal of things in the most nonchalant manner with whoever is willing to listen. And someone always is. There is no concept of *tznius* — of the importance of guarding the inner self from public exposure. Not everything which happens, even if it is true, is a fitting topic for public discussion. It can be demeaning to human dignity. It can be *assur* — forbidden — too.

Even the style of our speech says something about us. Our language is a mirror into our soul. Soft, genteel language is usually indicative of sensitive, refined people; coarse, loud, aggressive language is not. Shlomo *Hamelech* spoke about that too: *divrei chachamim b'nachas nishmaim* — the words of the wise are serenely spoken.

❧ ❧ ❧

So women of the world, rise up in pure, pristine speech! As you continue your verbal journey through life, talk, sing, teach; discuss, chat, parley; review, converse, confab! Your colloquial discourses are the oil which keeps the social machine humming, the thread which binds society together.

One note of caution: Just make sure you watch your tongue.

# A Most Modest Image

ow would you describe yourself? Modestly attractive? Attractively modest? Or not all that attractive but trying your best to get there ... in a modest manner, of course?

Whatever your answer, if you are being at all honest, you'll probably end up in hot water. And it's not your fault. For of all the many, detailed, clearly defined, black-and-white issues in Jewish custom and law, *tznius* is one area where it's awfully gray.

*Hechsheirim, chalav yisrael, glatt* meat and schools are always in the limelight. *Shemitah, shatnez, lashon hara* are carefully studied and discussed. *Muktzeh, tefillin,* the laws of *aveilus* merit clear rabbinical pronouncements. But who is around to explain the subtleties of *tznius,* and to decide whether or not that lovely black dress you saw this afternoon with the chic lines and the silver insets is appropriate clothing for today's Jewish female?

And who understands or thinks about or empathizes with the Jewish girl or woman trying hard to look both attractive and proper at the same time? How does one manage to look fashionable and chic without being overly visible? For isn't visibility what *tznius* is all about — not calling excessive (how much is "excessive"?) attention to ourselves in public?

We all know the laws well enough — what gets covered and what need not. But when it comes to fashion, *halachah* is not always enough, for the *how,* and not only the *how much,* becomes crucial. *How* do we attain a modicum of outward style without forfeiting the inner beauty and quiet *chein* which is the hallmark of the Jewish woman?

Think of wigs. Is a long, free-flowing wig, the kind that makes you look glamorous (you hope), OK? It does cover your hair; or can your hair be "overcovered"?

And what about accessories? There are thin, elegant high heels which make you feel like a princess (even if they do hurt after fifteen or twenty minutes — beauty has its price!) and shiny, sheer nylons (or the netted, lacy, spangled or otherwise decorated kind . . . as your taste may run). And the belts . . . wide, low-slung and saucy. If they're in style and we like them (even if they are a bit eye-catching), is there any reason not to buy them? Since when is a belt immodest attire?

And jewelry. How many rings or earrings or bracelets or necklaces or pins may a woman wear? It's true that sometimes we become a little like the lady in the nursery rhyme ("with rings on her fingers and bells on her toes"), but is being tinkly or shiny bad for the Jews? Diamonds and gold spread light and good cheer, and who's to say how much of a good thing is too much?

And last but not least, if the cosmetics industry is spending several billion dollars a year to keep us wrinkle free, moisturized, perfumed; colored, curled, blushed; polished, waxed, pencilled, shadowed and creamed; powdered, puffed, lacquered, painted, combed, teased, fresh smelling and sprayed, who are we small, insignificant creatures to swim against such a tidal wave of beautification?

Not long ago, we were limited. There was a partial cosmetic rest on the seventh day of the week. But now that *halachically* permissible *Shabbos* cosmetics are on the market, we can strive for total weekly beauty. The only remaining question is, should we?

The striving for beauty, for fashion, for attractiveness is as old as the first woman. Did not *Hakadosh Baruch Hu* Himself adorn Chavah as a bride? Did not Ezra have peddlers bring cosmetics to Jewish women to beautify themselves for their husbands? Does the *halachah* not require that a Jewish man purchase a gift of clothing for his wife on each *chag?* So what's all the fuss about?

But fuss there is. A constant, everyday struggle among sensitive, thinking women as we start each morning with *Modeh Ani* and then start wondering what to wear.

Most aggravating of all, it's hard for us to fool ourselves. We do try to look good, we know when we succeed, and we're aggravated when we don't. Being attractive is important to us. Is that wrong?

No, it's not wrong. There is a good reason why we are this way. Woman's desire to look attractive is part of G-d's comprehensive plan for the world, and as such, it plays an important part in keeping the race alive. But keeping it within bounds is hard work.

Compounding this difficulty is the universal human appreciation for and response to beauty. A love of beautiful things is found in all cultures, in all times, in all places. But the minute you add Decoration or Things Beautiful to Female, there you are, bumping into all those *tznius* problems again. Where does all this leave us, aside from being confused?

Fortunately, we do have certain guidelines. One is the word

"too." Not to be too fashionable, too chic, too made-up, too bejeweled. As long as we meet all of the clear *halachic* requirements, and then refrain from getting carried away by the seasonal dictates of contemporary fashion, we can hope to stay out of trouble.

Secondly, we possess a treasure all our own — an instinctive inner recording which echoes the voices of Sarah, Rivkah, Rachel, Leah, Yocheved, Miriam, Devorah, Chanah, and all the generations of worthy Jewish women who preceded us. If we hone our instincts and learn to hear and listen to these precious voices, and if we combine them with a little common sense and some individual good taste, we can hope to tread that fine line between being overly attractive and underly modest.

It's not an easy thing to do, and no one out there is offering us much useful advice. But then again, it's not the first time that Jewish women were left to their own devices, to combat their own problems, to find their own solutions. They usually do it quietly and out of the limelight too. It's more *tzniusdik* that way.

# The Jewish Woman's
# Guilt Chart

(Alphabetically Arranged for Easy Reference)

ANGER: An absolute no-no. *Chazal* say that one who loses his temper is akin to an idol-worshiper.

BIKUR CHOLIM: How come I never get around to visiting the *choleh* until he or she has usually recovered? There must be a logical explanation. I always have such good intentions.

COPING: I do, most of the time. It's the times I don't that vex me.

COOKING, CREATIVE: I don't, much. My mother did, a lot. Which makes me wonder where I went wrong.

DAUGHTERS, TEEN-AGE: Often difficult. Charming, wonderful, lovely, but definitely difficult. Is it my fault?

DISHES, DIRTY, IN THE SINK: Good housekeepers don't have them. I am a good housekeeper. So why. . . oh, never mind.

DUST, ALL OVER: Where does it all come from? And why doesn't it go back there?

EGO: It's always there, getting in the way.

ENERGY: I'm not so old. Why don't I have more of it?

FRIVOLOUS READING: I know it's a waste of time and I know it's stupid and beneath me and I know I could find something better to read if I only tried. But after a long, hard day, a little frivolous reading is *so* relaxing.

GOSSIP: I do not gossip. Gossiping is crude and forbidden and good people don't do it. I only discuss important things, which really do need discussing. And, of course, in a constructive way. (So why do I feel so guilty after my constructive discussions?)

HANG-UPS: How many have I caused or bequeathed to my poor, unsuspecting kids?

HACHNASAS ORCHIM: I do have guests, despite what my kids say. It's just that they think the house should be Grand Hotel every *Shabbos,* but I am tired, and enough is enough. I'm entitled to a quiet *Shabbos* once in a while, am I not?

IRONING: It just so happens that I enjoy ironing. But I don't say so out loud. It makes for enemies. Like when I mention that I iron my husband's and sons' shirts. All of them; every week. Some women don't. For shame. (So I'm feeling a little superior . . . so what?)

JEWELRY: I know that jewelry is superficial, vain and silly — mere playthings for women who are not really serious about life. (So who says you have to be serious all the time?)

KAVANAH: How is one supposed to *daven* with *kavanah* in the house, when the phone keeps ringing and people keep coming to the door to sell you something? Sometimes I wonder if I should go to the early *minyan* with my husband. (Do they *daven* with more *kavanah* there?)

LEARNING, MY HUSBAND'S: How many more hours a week could he learn if I would let him, and how come I don't ?

MENUS: How long can one keep making the same food? I must get myself some new recipes before the family turns into a tuna casserole.

MONEY: There's no keeping up with the Cohens in our house. Which is why I don't understand what all the fuss was about when I merely suggested buying a new dining room set.

NOISE & NEIGHBORS: It is extremely difficult to love your neighbors when their kids come equipped with automatic sound effects and exceedingly loud noise accessories.

NUDGING: An activity I often engage in. I'd love to stop. Any suggestions towards attaining this goal will be greatly appreciated.

OVEN: One of my recurring dreams used to be that the inside of mine was spotlessly clean. So I bought one that does the job. All by itself. (Am I superfluous now?)

PATIENCE: It is a virtue. Yes, indeed. But it takes so long to develop it!

PESACH: I admit it. I gave up by the time I reached the last cabinet in the kitchen. I cleaned it, but not with the same zeal that the first hundred cabinets, drawers and shelves received. So now I'm left with eight days of wondering: Is all the *chametz* really out?

QUARRELING: It really never pays and chances are you're in the wrong. (Sometimes, even when you're right, you're wrong.) So why not stop it before it starts?

RESTING: An activity I find extremely therapeutic at all times. So why do I always feel as though I am wasting time, when what I am actually doing is garnering energy?

REHASHING: As in arguments. Very bad habit. If you didn't make your point on the first round, chances are you won't make it on the second round either.

SHIURIM: There are so many around. Everyone goes. I should go too.

SHOPPING: Wouldn't it be nice if we could shorten the time necessary for shopping each week and use the free time for walking in the park? I know shopping is necessary and all that, but the park is so much more enjoyable. . .

SILLY SHOPPING: As opposed to the above, it is not necessary, and it's much more fun. I wonder why the things that are fun are so rarely necessary and the things that are necessary are so rarely fun.

SINGLE SOCKS: Where do they all come from? They all had partners when they entered the washing machine.

TALKING: I wish I did less. It often gets me into trouble. I also get tired of hearing myself. Which makes me wonder what the rest of my family and friends are thinking.

TIME: How I wish I had more of it and used what I had more constructively. . .

TZEDAKAH: I give conscientiously, almost all of the time. So why do I still feel that I'm not giving enough?

TZITZIS: Like Single Socks (see above), these too are a laundry-related problem. I *never* put *tzitzis* into the washer. Yet each week, at least one pair finds its way into the belly of the machine and is torn and tangled beyond repair. I *know* this is not my fault! Perhaps this is one problem I can safely remove from my guilt chart. It just may belong to the men in our house.

UPS & DOWNS: My emotional states. Life would be much easier if I regulated my U's & D's more successfully.

VANITY: Generally and unjustly ascribed to women. But men are just as vain, and anyway, isn't it a *mitzvah* for a woman to keep herself attractive for her husband? It's not her fault if other people happen to see her too.

WEIGHT, ADDITIONAL AND UNWANTED: If G-d wanted all women to be skinny, He'd have made them that way. Besides, a mature women shouldn't look like a scarecrow. Right?

X: The world's sign for a kiss. Why did I insist that my five-year-old go to sleep without the last kiss he wanted? So what if it was the seventh one he asked for? Maybe he just needs my love.

YELLING: Civilized, intelligent people do not yell. They do not lose their temper or their cool or their control. Yelling is futile. It is damaging to the yeller and to the "yellee." As a civilized, intelligent person, I do not yell. I only raise my voice because the people I am speaking to are not listening.

# Families
## are Forever

*Families are forever, or they're supposed to be. But even when the threads that keep families together unravel a bit, the bond of biology is still strong. Despite the many strains and stresses inherent in groups of diverse people living in long, close proximity, the family is still the primary force that molds and holds people and civilizations together.*

*Having been established and having received their charters, so to speak, from the Creator Himself, families are endowed with Divine functions and responsibilities. When these are satisfactorily fulfilled, happy, healthy, productive people and a better world are the final result.*

*This, of course, is why we are so concerned with the type of family our kids marry into. No one is an island, and in some measure, everyone is influenced by the family he comes from. And everyone — island or not! — deserves to be surrounded by a sea of familial love and affection. We have yet to discover or invent a substitute which nurtures and educates and encourages the best in human beings as does the everyday, commonplace, ordinary family.*

*Every family is a world unto itself. They come in varying sizes, colors, shapes, sounds, and designs. They exist in different economic brackets, live in widely diverse geographical locations, and are clothed in a myriad of civilizations and styles. Yet, like the people they contain, families are enough alike so that we can love, enjoy, or be exasperated by tales of them all. Which is why you will probably find a few familiar tales, reminiscent of your own family, on the following pages. Enjoy!*

# Fruitful Multiplication

dding is simple. You take two or more existing items, put them side by side, and count them. Multiplying is more complicated, as any set of parents can tell you. Yet multiplication is what it's all about. It's a *mitzvah;* it's a blessing; and it's heartwarming and housewarming as well. For those products of the multiplication process fill homes and hearts with the enduring warmth of love.

Baby Love is probably the purest, strongest and most instinctive form of love around. It brings out the best in us — patience, tenderness and pity. Lots of self-sacrifice too, just about knocking aside all of our usual egocentric concerns. Because of their vulnerability and great need, we care for our babies as if our lives depended on it. Theirs certainly do.

This must be the reason why we'll patiently zoom-zoomy

each spoonful of food into a messy little mouth (Note: "zoom-zoomy" is a local eating-sound which accompanies and facilitates child-feeding.) Or why we'll crawl around on all fours barking like a dog or roaring like a lion for the edification of some two or three year old. Or why we'll build and rebuild endless towers which baby keeps knocking down, sing and re-sing endless silly songs, read and reread the same story a zillion times, just because the pint-sized creature in front of us takes delight in our doing so.

It's worth it too, every zoom-zoomy, song, tower and story. For what other creature represents such a fantastic enterprise? Here is a unique partnership between G-d and two human beings. A grand *mitzvah* and major investment with, *b'ezras Hashem,* a glowing future in store.

But babies are more than just private property. There is a public side to them as well. Each baby represents a communal asset; a link in the chain of *Klal Yisrael* — the Jewish People. And each contains a bit of eternity, equipped as it is with our parents' eyes, noses, chins; our grandparents' hands, fingers, smiles; our uncles' and aunts' expressions; plus a combination of qualities from countless unknown ancestors. A magnificent work of wisdom and art — that's what our kids are — brought into being by an unbeatable trio: Mommy, Daddy, and the Master Creator Himself.

❦  ❦  ❦

Nowadays, babies become crawlers who develop into toddlers who then graduate into pre-schoolers who become just plain children, after which they are known as teenagers. Once, long ago, they became children immediately, just as once, there was no such thing as a teen. But now that we have progressed, we have divided things up more efficiently.

When families are blessed with additional children, the children become siblings. Unfortunately, many of the books and studies and magazines articles about siblings have given brothers and sisters a bad name. (I just hear the word sibling, and "rivalry" lights up like a neon sign in my mind.) I will admit that with the proliferation of siblings in a family, there does tend to be a certain proliferation of work and problems, but it's not anywhere nearly as bad as the psychologists would have us think.

A sister or a brother means love, not hostility. Friends, not only fights. The excitement of learning and growing together, not just competing. Where else can you find an intimate, lifelong friend and buddy who shares so much of your life? Who speaks the same language, laughs at the same jokes, understands and perhaps possesses your particular strengths and weaknesses, values and opinions? Where else will you find such an open door, heart, and (usually) pocket? Some-one who will share your *simchahs,* and *chas v'chalilah,* your sorrows so sincerely? Someone who, if he or she only can, will be there in your hour of need?

So what if you argued for years over who got the bed by the window? Your brother *kvelled* with *nachas* and was absolutely thrilled when you won the Best Student Award at your graduation.

And that sister you fought with tooth and nail — the one who was always in your drawers and borrowing your clothes without permission — just had her first baby. And she looks like you! You couldn't love that child more if it were your own (which, in a way, it is).

I remember an eight-year-old son carrying his younger brother home in his arms one day. The younger one had fallen from a bicycle and had a nasty split on his forehead. He was covered with blood, but his older brother was chalk white, trembling with fear and worry. His state of shock was at least as serious as his brother's need for stitches.

And years later, when their five-year-old sister spent a few days in the hospital after a rather frightening infection, all her brothers rearranged their schedules and divided the day into shifts so someone could be at her side, twenty-four hours a day. A few days later, when I suggested that she could be safely left alone for a few hours (by then she was feeling fine and having a wonderful time with the other kids in the room), her brothers were appalled. Sure that I had lost my senses, they continued to stand guard at her bed around the clock.

Today, years later, she alternately mothers and bosses and bothers and teases them, while they give as well as they get — a sure sign that love reigns supreme.

The daughter of a friend also comes to mind. After waiting many years for a bedroom of her own, she finally got one when the house "emptied out" after the marriage of several brothers. My friend plastered, painted and prettied up the empty bedroom, turning a boy's fortress into a girl's frilly, pink boudoir. But for months, the room remained empty as Daughter continued to sleep with her other brothers and sisters. She moved all of her things into the new room, did her homework there, brought her friends there to play. But at night, she returned to her old bedroom. No, she wasn't afraid to sleep alone; she was simply lonely. You see, there was no one to talk to or laugh with in the lovely, new room. The love and the laughter were obviously worth more than the decor.

"When all is said and done," said a man we know, "a family is like a bank. Every member is an invaluable asset. Increase the ones you can and hang onto all the rest. The more you have, the wealthier you are."

# The Worrying Mode

 know that people are supposed to adapt, to be flexible, to change as they grow, and I don't think I'm any less pliable than the next person. But it's hard to change a lifetime pattern just because the little people you developed the pattern for in the first place grew so much bigger. And it seems to me that desirable qualities and habits should remain desirable, even if the size of the recipient (read: offspring) changes somewhat.

Yet I have found that certain universal, basic mothering traits — traits which served me and my children well for many years — have now been declared obsolete. Two such items on the disposal list prepared by our kids are the dual traits of Worrying and Checking. (To be effective, Worrying must be accompanied by Checking. Not the bank book kind of checking; the Making Sure kind.)

For example: Did you eat? Where's the button that fell off your sweater yesterday? Don't forget your dentist appointment! Are all your dirty clothes in the hamper? Did you find your umbrella? It's cold! Wear your coat! Do you have enough money? Did someone take the garbage out?

These are, in my opinion, elementary questions designed to keep an individual on top of things, the type of checking that keeps a household running smoothly. Just imagine what chaos would result if no one kept track of uneaten meals, loose buttons, dentist appointments, laundry, lost umbrellas, and garbage! Any sane, orderly mind reels at the thought of it.

Yet, as children (the category of people who usually need this type of checking the most!) grow older, they seem to consider these basic housekeeping functions an attack on their integrity, an insult to their good character, and an intrusion on their privacy. And the older they grow, the more resentful they become.

Nor is the average offspring satisfied with trying to limit his or her parent's checking reflex. They try to change the very thought processes which are the basis for effective worrying.

"Don't worry so much!" they tell you glibly. (As if anything would ever work out if I didn't worry about it.) "I'll manage fine." (I've heard that one before.) "I'm not hungry now. I'll take my own food later." (Tell me all about it in half an hour, after the food is all gone and the kitchen is all clean.) "Of course all my dirty socks are in the hamper. Where else would they be?" (Back in your drawer?) "I don't need a coat. It's not cold!" (I'm already writing out a check for the doctor and the antibiotics.)

You see, I'm not conjecturing. I *know* that cough is one step before bronchitis. I *know* that it's going to pour in half an hour. I *know* you will be dead tired for that test or will miss the last bus or will come home without your umbrella again. These are facts, not mere opinions; irrefutable, concrete facts. I have not spent the past twenty-five years of my life arranging, fixing, worrying and checking for nothing. I have it all down to a science, and believe me, if I worry about something, there's good reason for it.

In addition to all the above-mentioned minor worries, there are the biggies to think about, too. Will we all stay healthy? Will the kids, and their kids, and the as-yet-unborn kids, all marry and have children (who will be healthy and marry and have children. . .) and live happily ever after? Will everyone make a living? Will there be peace? Will the man come to fix the washing machine at ten o'clock as he promised so that I won't miss the meeting with Moishe's teacher again? Someone has to think about these things.

I try to be persistent and persevering, following faithfully in the footsteps of my mother, an expert, experienced worrier of the previous generation. In our youthful ignorance, we would sometimes laugh and call her Cassandra — the ancient Greek prophetess of doom and gloom. Cassandra was always expecting the worst, and she was usually right, a fact my mother never neglected to point out.

My friend's mother was also a great worrier. My friend once said her mother's head was full of worry slots, and as soon as one emptied out, her mother immediately filled it with a fresh, new worry so that the slots would always remain full. I had this mental image of her mother's brain divided into little, square cubbyholes, each one filled with a neat, rolled up worry.

Yet despite these fond memories laden with wisdom, I close my eyes, hold my ears, and shut my mouth, trying hard not to think about or mention the worrisome things fluttering around my brain. Then, after not mentioning at least forty-six important items, one slips through, and I'm immediately greeted by the same old family chorus: Worrying again?

On the other hand, if I ever decide (and on special occasions, I do) that I'm retired, independent, and disconnected from some particular family affair, I find that I'm still accountable for all that follows.

"Isn't there anything left to eat?" "You could have saved me something!" "It did cost more than I thought after all." "Can you give me some money?" "Where are all my socks?" "Didn't you do the laundry this week?" "Of course I didn't go to the dentist; I thought you canceled the appointment!" "It's the garbage that smells. I forgot to take it out last night, but you're going out now. Can you take it?" And yes, the cough did turn out to be a bad case of bronchitis.

My eldest (himself a father) once asked me when I would finally stop worrying.

"Stop worrying?" I answered in a mature, serious tone of voice — the kind that only years of life experience can bestow. "Worrying comes with giving birth. It's part and parcel of motherhood. Do you want to deprive me of my maternal birthright? In the World to Come, I'll stop worrying. On second thought, I probably won't stop then either. I'll have your great-grandchildren to think about. Haven't you ever heard of a *malitz yosher* — someone to put in a good word for you with G-d?"

He had, but he didn't think it had any connection with worrying. But then again, he doesn't really understand. I've found that fathers and sons often don't. To appreciate the full extent of maternal worry — its unending and comprehensive character — one has to be a mother. Worrying, at least in our house, is definitely a feminine specialty.

# The Later Syndrome

or me, the three or four worst days in the year are the post-cleaning but pre-Pesach days. The kitchen is all *Pesachdik,* but the family stomachs aren't. These are the Days of Hunger when the *yom tov* cooking is bubbling on the stove and there is neither time nor place nor wherewithal to cook any more *chametz.* It is also the time when the family suddenly develops an intense longing for bread-related food. Nothing else will stave off the famine. You'd think there wasn't a thing in the world to eat besides spaghetti, toast, pizza or falafel in a good chewy pita!

I banish the eaters to the porch, no matter what the weather. They have had their pre-Pesach meals on our porch in rain and shine, fanning themselves in broiling *chamsinim* and bundled up in winter coats in frigid temperatures. Hot or cold, wet or dry, the view is great. There, exposed to the elements, they can eat whatever they like, as long as it doesn't have to be cooked in my beautifully *Pesachdika* kitchen. All dirty dishes are rerouted to the bathroom for washing and Heaven help the person who unthinkingly leaves a *chametzdika* glass in my sparkling *Pesachdika* sink!

I wait nervously for the day of redemption. Not Pesach, but *erev* Pesach, when all *chametz* must be disposed of and the porch can finally join the rest of the house in a state of purification. Then, and only then, will I be able to relax, knowing that all is clean and ready for the *chag*. There will no longer be any danger of *chametz* contamination, because there will no longer be any *chametz*!

But before we reach that blessed state of affairs, there are several last-minute things to be done. And at these final preparatory stages which will brook no delay, I inevitably encounter what I call the "Not Now, Later" syndrome. I shall attempt to explain.

We all know that "Now" is the sign of the child. You know . . . no patience, instant gratification. (I once heard this marvelous song about a little boy who is supposed to have gone to sleep but who keeps calling, "MOMMMMY! Gimm-meeee a drink o' waaater! Not later, Mommy! NOW, Mommy, NOW!")

I don't think of myself as a child, but I find I am often under the influence of the Now, and I think it's absolutely justified. Especially on *erev Shabbos* and *erev yom tov*. And extra especially on *erev* Pesach.

As I'm hurrying to get those last crumbs off the porch, I find that my daughter has suddenly discovered our floor tiles. All those layers of wax we put on the floor throughout the year have built up (so she says) and the floor looks yellow (funny I never noticed it), but she has found that using a paint scraper takes it all off. (We once tried using ammonia, but it ate holes in the tiles and left a piece of the floor looking like an eroded moonscape.)

So there she is, my mainstay, my helper, my right-hand Pesach cleaner, down on her knees happily scraping away, tile by tile, six hours before the *Seder*. (We have approximately 2400 floor tiles in the house.)

"Forget the tiles!" I cry. "If you must scrape something, scrape something sensible like the table and chairs!"

"Not now," she tells me. "Soon."

Soon? When is Soon on *erev* Pesach? "Do it now," I plead. But she's in a trance, steadily advancing across the floor, tile by tile.

"We'll be able to eat off the floors on *yom tov*," I say, "but not off the kitchen table. Please . . . let the floors alone. You can do them next month, or next year. Or before you get married. There are other, more important things to do now!"

"Don't worry," she reassures me. "It'll all get done. Later!"

"I know, I know," I cry. "But I don't want you scrubbing my kitchen table later. We'll be in the middle of the *Seder* later. Do it NOW, not later, NOW!"

※　※　※

This kind of thing happens other times as well. On *erev Shabbos* I like the table set in the morning. It makes me feel happy and *Shabbosdik* all day Friday. There's nothing wrong with that, is there? But my kids think there is.

"Not now, later," they say. Week after week. "It'll get done before you light the candles. Don't worry."

I know it will, and I'm not worrying. I just want the table set. NOW.

I guess it has to do with one's priorities. I have a certain internal timetable and sense of order, and it seems to me that it's easier and pleasanter and more logical to do things my way. But I'm obviously a majority of one.

Sometimes I'll take the "Not now, later" route myself. But if I do, it's because I know that it really *doesn't* matter if something gets put off. (No one in the house cares much if I make my phone calls or vacuum first — not unless they want the phone.) But I suppose that's what the kids are saying too — it doesn't make a difference if the floor is washed or the table set or a phone call made right now or a little later. It'll get done by the time it has to.

Who knows? Maybe they're right. Maybe it's a better idea to quit nudging and let everyone work according to his or her own personal schedule. As they say, in the end, it will get done. And if I'm not happy with their speedometers, I can always go and do the thing myself. That way, it gets done. Now.

# Surviving the Summer Virus

very year, as spring blooms its way into summer, an annual virus blooms its way into unsuspecting homes across the country. Once inside, it whispers innocently, "And where shall we go this year?"

The wise have learned to ignore it, but most of us simple people are inevitably infected. Thinking, as we erringly do, that the Family Vacation is an integral part of the responsibility of raising children, we succumb. The maps emerge, the suitcases are *shlepped* up from the basement, the car is brought in for a general check-up, and after a frenzied round of summer purchases, the family piles into the well-packed, gas-filled wagon or van and we're off.

It's an exhilarating sensation, that first hour or two, with the wind blowing through your hair, the road stretching out before you, the children singing happily behind you and all your everyday troubles temporarily forgotten. It lasts until the five-year-old needs a bathroom.

After fifteen or so years of summer vacations, we can provide travelers with an up-to-date road map of every usable bathroom in Israel. Of course my mother used to say that she had visited every single usable bathroom in downtown Chicago with us when we were young, so I suppose I have no cause to complain.

Then there's the Throw-up Brigade. All they have to do is sit down in the car and they're already feeling nauseous. A well-organized family is always equipped with plastic bags.

The car has to be stroked and thought of, too, despite the pristine condition in which it began its journey. The mishaps we have experienced over the years sound like a litany of demise. A fan belt broke while going up a steep mountain incline; a leaking radiator left us in the desert with a roasting motor on a broiling day, far from the nearest service station; tires went flat by sunlight and moonbeams; horns have gone haywire and wires have crossed and short-circuited the whole operation in mid-journey. All this, mind you, after the car was checked out and pronounced whole and healthy.

*Tefillas Haderech,* an integral part of every trip, is always recited slowly and out loud. The roads are, for many reasons, not always a sympathetic place to be, and at a very young age, our kids already knew exactly where, once out of the city limits, *Tefillas Haderech* had to be recited.

Israeli trips tend to be "*tiyulim,*" which means that once you've safely arrived at your destination, you are not yet there. "There" means the hiking, climbing, scrambling, swimming, and otherwise strenuous activities you are indulging in for your rest and relaxation. Israeli children are not interested in simply "seeing" the Land. In order to tour it, they have to physically walk through it (driving will not do), climb up it and slide down it to get the proper feel of the thing.

Therefore, when our kids were small, we had rules which had to be strictly upheld, which they were . . . until they were forgotten. Then something unexpected, some situation you couldn't have dreamed of if you tried, would crop up.

For example, there was the charming, quiet, organized, family (which meant: for children) hike. It was sponsored by the Israel Nature Society and was to be an easy, three-hour walk through part of the Judean desert. I had relaxed the You Must Hold My Hand The Entire Way! rule because the boys were up front with the guide, holding his hand (or so I thought). Bringing up the rear (my usual position on hikes), I came across our group gathered anxiously at a deep rift, where a narrow aqueduct, serving as a bridge, stretched to the other side. There they all stood, some in stunned silence while others loudly steered a child across the bridge.

"Slow now! Easy does it! Don't look down!"

I did, though, and I saw my son hanging under the aqueduct, holding on for dear life with his hands. He had chosen to cross this way because, as he later said, the aqueduct was full of water, and if he would have walked on top of it and through it (as everyone else was doing) he would have gotten his shoes wet. (This was the first time I ever noticed that he cared about wet shoes.) And so he swung his way across the rift manually, the deep desert chasm gaping under him, but keeping his dirty, torn, old gym shoes dry. Tarzan never had such problems.

After he reached the other side and they got my heart going again, I held his little hand tightly in my own and dragged him through the rest of the afternoon. He screamed all the way. (He didn't want to hold my hand. He wanted to go up front again with the guide.)

We had another water-related heart stopper with one of our friend's children. This live-wire had slipped into the water (and I would not joke about a thing like this) at the top of a high, rocky waterfall. As everyone stood around admiring the beautiful, swiftly flowing stream approaching its steep, picturesque drop, my husband saw something which did not look at all like a fish swoosh by. Fortunately he grabbed it in time, a deed which allowed us to attend the unwitting diver's wedding around fifteen years later. *Baruch Hashem!*

Not all vacations are this exciting, however, which is a problem in itself. As the kids get older, they divide into two types. Type A's script reads: It's boring here. What is there to do? If you suggest that everyone just sit back and enjoy the scenery, you get a repeat. It's boring here. . .

Type B is the Already Done It gang. Wherever you go, whatever you do, they tell you: I don't wanna go there again. We already saw that last year. So it was two years ago, but it still looks the same. . .

And when the kids are finally old enough so that you can enjoy their company and you want to be with them, they don't want to go with you at all. They go off to camp, to be with their friends. You have to wait until they've married and produced kids of their own for them to return for a family vacation (with Bubby and Zeidy usually footing the bill). At that point, you may not be so sure *you* can relax and enjoy while keeping track of the new Diaper Brigade!

But in spite of it all, I must admit that every summer the virus returns and does its work. We even try to infect our friends and relatives so that we'll have company on our journey. Warm weather makes us restless and the call of the country is strong. So we check out the car, bring up the suitcases, and pack some food. And we're off again.

# An Unpolished Diamond:

## The Trials and Tribulations of Raising a Teen-Age Daughter

 didn't really believe them when they told me. Even though they were good friends, intelligent, thinking women with experience in this sort of thing. But it all sounded so silly, so full of cliches; I was sure they were just exaggerating. It didn't hit home until I realized that I couldn't get a line anymore. On my own phone too. The one my husband and I pay for with our hard-earned money.

The phone, you see, was always busy. I had to beg her to finish her conversations so I could make some emergency call, for example, before they closed the office I happened to need. And after a minute or two, I'd find myself apologizing. "I'm almost through. Just one more second and you can have the phone back. I know I interrupted your conversation. I'll be through in a minute . . ."

It was obvious that if I didn't free the line for the long, lithe and lovely young creature standing at my elbow, some global catastrophe would immediately ensue. Perhaps she and her best friend who lives across the street (which is a good thing; otherwise they wouldn't survive the separation after school) were arranging a summit conference between Shamir and Hussein. Perhaps they were about to iron out some last-minute hitch in a new satellite waiting to be momentarily launched. Perhaps . . . my imagination ran dry. But whatever it was they were discussing, it was vital, immediate, and overwhelmingly important. Far beyond any of the trivial matters I mundanely engage in.

It really all took me by surprise. Perhaps because this was the first daughter after a row of sons. After a certain age, sons seem to spend less time around the house than a daughter does, so perhaps I didn't notice what was going on with them until it was over. In any event, as Daughter stood upon the threshold of young womanhood, I became aware of a new reality in our heretofore tranquil home.

I could no longer simply leave the house when I so desired. First I had to be inspected. And I never passed. "Oiy, Imma! Don't you have any other shoes? Those don't match your coat!" (Since when do my shoes have to match my coat?) "And please, wear your other *sheitel!* That one's a mess. And won't you put on a little lipstick? You look so pale."

*Shabbos* and *simchahs* were even worse. "Is that what you're going to wear? No one wears those sweaters anymore! Don't you have any pride in the way you look? If you don't care about yourself, at least think of me! What will my friends think when they see you?"

I looked at myself in the mirror. Not exactly the slender

beauty I was at twenty-one, but all things considered, definitely passable. My slip wasn't showing, my hem wasn't torn and there were no runs in my nylons. And my clothes matched, even if my shoes and my coat didn't. So what was so awful?

The strangest part of all was, that considering the dreadful condition of my wardrobe (according to my daughter), she was always asking to borrow something of mine because she had "nothing to wear."

Nor were clothes the only thing she didn't have. She didn't have any time either. Time to help clean or shop or bake or fold laundry. Because she was so busy with other things which were more important. Her homework and music and art and sewing lessons and good deeds for people who "really need them" kept her busy, busy, busy. If she had to put in some house-helping time once in a while, she always seemed to get her good-natured brother to share it with her the minute he came home from the yeshivah.

Speaking of brothers, communication with them was often faulty. It consisted of insults (loving or otherwise), complaints and commands (which they ignored with great aplomb). Perhaps she was just out of practice in the use of verbal communication with siblings because so much of her time was spent with her best friend. Fortunately, because Best Friend lived across the street, time not spent with her could nonetheless be spent keeping in touch via the windows and over the expanse of the street. This was very helpful if someone in the house was inadvertently tying up the telephone line.

Food was another problematic topic. Daughter was always starving, but she could not (would not?) cook. If she was forced to prepare an omelet once in a while, she wanted to know why there was "never anything to eat in this house." Perhaps the reason was because the eaters consumed the food faster than the shoppers and cookers could replace it!

Then there were the shoes. In every room. If a person owns three pairs of shoes, a pair of houseslippers and a pair of boots, it must take great concentration to manage to have each and every shoe, slipper and boot separated from its mate and in a different room. But she managed it without batting an eyelash. Or a shoestring. And when asked why the house had to look like such a mess, and exactly when would she learn how to be more orderly, she answered without hesitation that when *she* got married, *her* house would be spotless and lovely.

All of the above, however, was trivial in comparison to the issue of shopping. Clothes shopping. Living as we do in Israel, where the concept of returning goods and receiving a refund is virtually unknown, shopping takes on gargantuan importance, for any purchase you have made is now eternally yours. At best, you may possibly exchange it for some other item in the store. Considering the price of clothes in Israel (sometimes double to triple the price of clothing in the U.S.), shopping is no longer a "fun" thing. It's serious business.

So girls normally shop with their mothers to make sure that what they are buying is what they want, for once they've bought it, it's theirs. And the suffering inflicted upon all concerned is undoubtedly an atonement for our many sins. Patience, fortitude and tact will, of course, make the experience more bearable. Especially if it's the mother who is displaying them.

🦋 🦋 🦋

HOWEVER . . . lest you think, (even for one tiny moment!) that our female offspring was anything less than a source of great *nachas* and joy (*biz ah hundred un tzvanzig!*) let me now inform you that you simply do not sufficiently comprehend how charming, how loving, how kind, sensitive and wonderful a creature a teen-age daughter can be.

Who else would leave you little notes to greet you when

you wake up in the morning? And who else would overcome a deep, innate aversion to dead chickens and make *Shabbos* when you get sick on Friday morning? (It was all pretty good, too!) Who else would fill your home with beautiful music as she sits for hours practicing whatever it is she plays without your even having to nudge? (Any daughter who is still playing an instrument at this age is playing for the love of it, not because her mother thinks she has to.)

And just imagine . . . she sewed! And with more patience (whoever thought she would ever do something patiently?) and more skill than her mother commands. The things she made were even wearable when she finished!

And best of all, that absent-minded child whom you thought would never learn the multiplication tables or remember which books she needed for school on which days made her way cheerfully through high school with hardly a complaint from the educational powers that be. Her marks were fine, her books in order, and her enthusiasm high. And when, on occasion, the clouds did come rolling in, she had the wherewithal to sit down and work things out to a satisfactory conclusion.

How young and naive and eager they are — these fresh, young women. And how sincerely they try to do what's good and right, to live up to the teachings of their mothers and fathers, even when they try to do it *their* way. How easy it is to see them as the mothers of a new generation, doing a job every bit as good as their mothers before them.

Meanwhile, each night, I still stop at the door of her room to smile a goodnight and blow her a kiss after she's asleep. In my mind's eye, I can already see her doing the same for her daughter.

# Absent Offspring

ll normal mothers love their children equally — short or tall, fat or skinny, light-complexioned or dark, noisy or quiet, and of course, male or female. No matter what colors, kinds, sizes or emotional dispositions they come in, we take them to our hearts and spend some twenty-odd years (or more) providing an unending supply of food, love, clean clothing and advice. Fortunately, a certain set of basic, common-sense rules can be applied to raising all sorts of children; otherwise, our efforts to turn these widely varying creatures into *"mentshen"* would be immeasurably more complicated.

Nonetheless, it's as plain as day that there are certain very essential differences between certain kinds of children — mostly between the boy and girl varieties — and certain very basic differences in the way we're supposed to deal with them. When *Hakadosh Baruch Hu* created the world, He divided everything up into *"minnim"* — different kinds and species — and when He does a job, He does it well, which goes to explain why these differences between the sexes are so basic and enduring.

All of this might be inconsequential, except for one thing. Mothers and daughters, being of the same "kind", usually share a common telepathic state. Even when they argue and disagree, there is an instinctive, rock-bottom understanding of how the other one's mental and psychic processes work (which is probably why they can argue so long and well — each has a good feel for the other's weak points).

On the other hand, mothers and sons are often divided by an invisible, incomprehensible wall of non-communication, even when they are cooperating, loving, and on good terms. Let me explain.

A mother watching her daughter dress and undress a doll for two hours not only understands her daughter's activity; she also approves and empathizes. This is love, caring, giving, at the age-two level. A mother watching her son turn a single screw for two hours, or pushing a truck around in non-ending circles, or watching a bug take a nap on the floor, can also "understand." Her son is engaged in mental development, calculating, analyzing, constructing; but her heart isn't in it. She may, after the first ten minutes, begin wondering if he isn't overdoing it a bit. I mean, how long can you watch a bug? There is a limit. She cannot really empathize with what her son is doing because it's not the kind of thing she herself would ever do. While his activities may sometimes make sense to her brain, they do not necessarily speak to her soul.

The list is long. Acquiring an understanding of masculine interests and behavior patterns requires at least twenty years of effort by Mother. Little girls, and bigger ones, are basically talkative, affectionate, cozy, home-loving bodies whose home is the center of their universe. Even when they start their journey into the outside world, mother and home are at the core of their hearts.

On the other hand, little boys, as they grow older, often become less openly affectionate. (I stress the word "openly.") They seem less worried about parental love, more indepen- dent, more aggressive and very anxious to get out there, join the action, and conquer their piece of the world.

Little girls warm a mother's feminine heart. They take pride in pretty, clean new clothes, even though they may leave the house all nice and neat and return all messy, torn and soiled an hour later. Little boys don't seem to care one way or the other what you put on them.

(Note: If I sound blatantly sexist, perhaps it's because I am. I have yet to be convinced that there is no difference between little boys and little girls other than the physical differences. And I have *Chazal* to back me up!)

Little girls like songs and poems and presents and fancy parties; little boys like noise and jokes and lots of plain, good food. Little girls like to play Mommy. Little boys like to play Daddy, but not for long. Mostly, they like to run around and do things, in lots of space, with lots of noise and lots of action accompanying them.

But before a mother really has time to assimilate this information and rationally plan for a life of sons, before she has even finished folding their diapers and putting away their toys, they are suddenly away at school for most of the day. And when they come home after their long, tiring schedule, the last thing they have in mind is sitting still for a quiet, affectionate hour with Mommy. They need to get rid of some of that excess energy they've been storing up during school hours.

The next thing you know, they are off to yeshivah, possibly dorming away from home. Their rooms are empty; the clothes they've left behind stay neatly folded in the drawers; the house is strangely silent, listening for their particular sounds, even when sisters or younger brothers are still around. We begin to wonder — will they become mere holiday-summer visitors in their own home?

We are also left wondering — is he getting enough to eat in the yeshivah? Is he really happy? Perhaps the schedule is too rough for him, after all, he is so young. . . We wait for the letters and phone calls which arrive with maddening irregularity and inform us of the most irrelevant things. Even the questions they ask ("Did someone feed my fish?" "Did I get any mail?" "Ask Heshie to look for my green pen.") cause us to wonder — do they think of us or miss us at all? There is no doubt that we take pride and *"shep nachas"* from their learning and growing, but there is always that gnawing feeling beneath it all: someone else is educating, seeing, talking to, guiding and shaping my son on a daily basis now, not I. Sometimes, when we think about it, it's a little hard.

If you live in Israel, there is a plus, and a minus. "Going away to yeshivah" is less traumatic because the country is so small that kids are home more frequently. But on the other hand, you have an additional separation to incorporate into your life. If your son learns in a *hesder* yeshivah, he will also serve in the army. Once in, he is also answerable to his commander, not just to his parents.

It's true that previously he had to answer to his *rosh yeshivah* too, but somehow, *roshei yeshivah* and parents seem to be two different versions of one thing. Army commanders, on the other hand, while sympathetic to a serious family problem, are not very interested in your explaining that Moishe has a bad allergy to pollen and doesn't function too well for a few weeks in the spring. Unless Moishe becomes a hospital case, *chas v'chalilah,* he is going to have to overcome his spring discomfort and keep his act together, which is what the army is all about.

(And may I add, for those who have not had sons in the Israeli army, that when a parent thinks of the reason and need for the army, and of the possible activities their son might be engaged in, and given the great disinclination of young soldiers to discuss these activities with their parents so that you're often left wondering exactly what part did Moishe play in that little operation last week when his unit was sent out, an entire new dimension of worry is activated in the parental head and heart. It's a wonderful exercise in *bitachon* and *emunah,* although it would be even more wonderful if *Mashiach* arrived and it weren't necessary.)

Last but not least, the long-awaited day comes when you accompany your by-now-grown son down the aisle to the *chuppah.* What Jewish parent doesn't dream of this day? A new branch, a new *bayis,* a new generation — the realization of all your dreams. But where does this leave your son? Out of your house again, this time in a home of his own with a lovely, but virtually unknown, stranger! This, of course, is what marriage is all about, but nonetheless, it is another form of separation which needs adjusting to.

Yet our sons love us as strongly and as steadfastly as our daughters, even though they are less verbal, less openly affectionate, less physically attached to their parents' homes. Fathers, obviously, have less trouble tuning in to the masculine expression of love. Mothers must sometimes learn to adjust their sensitive antennae to the male mind in order to better hear and see what is in their sons' hearts.

Amazingly, we usually succeed. Perhaps, because we have practiced so long and so hard — on our sons' fathers.

# Books, Books, Books

 have, upon occasion, considered moving into a library, which is what our home resembles more and more from day to day. I figure one may as well live in the real McCoy instead of in a mere copy!

I'm a book person myself, and like to be surrounded by words printed and bound, rather than by the spoken type which tend to float around all over the place. Nonetheless, there's a limit to everything, including books.

When we moved into our present place of abode twenty-some years ago, I cleaned and organized and arranged and saw to it that there would be enough new bookshelves to house the family collection, plus some. But like the family, the books have since multiplied, and not finding enough space on the shelves with their friends, they have moved into halls, the kitchen, and the bedrooms. Some have even made the sad and difficult trip down to the storage room in the basement. The only place they are not found is in the living room, which I had insisted remain book-free.

This, I later discovered, almost broke up a *shidduch*. One of our daughters-in-law said that the first time she came to visit, she was struck by the fact that there were — I quote — "no books in the house." Not having been treated to a tour of the den, kitchen, halls and bedrooms, she had seen the only book-free area we have. Fortunately, before she was scared away, she got a glimpse of the study, which, *baruch Hashem*, saved the engagement.

Our books are slotted by rooms — Abba's *sifrei kodesh* go into the study; each kid's books go into his or her own room and are forever referred to as the books from So-and-So's room, even if they are eventually adopted by someone else and moved; Imma's *non-sifrei kodesh* books belong to the hall; cooking and health books are in the kitchen; etc.

Once on a shelf, a book retains its place only as long as it is used. When things begin to get crowded (as they always do) and a book doesn't seem to be in daily demand, it tends to get relegated to a somewhat hidden, second line of defense, in back of the front-line books. Which is fine, except that the result is: 1) awfully crowded bookshelves, and 2) if you ever want a back-line book, you have to start pulling things down and apart until you find it.

Pesach time is our Annual-Book Arranging Festival when everyone is expected to clean, make order, return books which aren't supposed to be there, and find the ones which are. Many interesting things, such as misplaced books, surface during Festival time.

The Longest-Misplaced-Book prize went to a juvenile novel with the name "Shmuli" inscribed inside. According to the reading level, it seemed to have come from one of our kid's friends at least ten years earlier. We hurriedly returned it (better late than never!) only to have it sent back the next day.

It's not their book, they said. Must belong to some other Shmuli. But theirs is the only Shmuli our son could think of. I am now left with pangs of guilt every time I see that particular book. I wonder — does little-Shmuli-now-grown-big think longingly of it when he passes his bookshelves? Has its place been filled by some other book, or does it still stand empty, waiting?

Pesach also sees the annual emptying of the Borrowed Book Shelf, as we return books which have been sitting around and shouldn't have been. We try hard to keep borrowed books together so that they don't get swallowed up among our books, as the unknown Shmuli's did. We also get a windfall of books into the house as other Pesach cleaners return the ones they borrowed from us. It's like Old Book Week, as we happily greet familiar covers and titles. I just wish people wouldn't send books back at the very last minute, after the bookcases are all cleaned and reorganized, because then we are stuck with finding place for the returnees on the already-full shelves.

In general, getting rid of excess books is a difficult business. Even moving them down to the basement involves a lot of soul searching. How can one possibly relinquish fifteen years of magazines? Or one's old school books? Even though one knows the chances of ever opening them up again are remote. But some day, one just may decide to review Ancient Semitic History, mayn't one? You never know.

I do think, however, that the younger generation should not clutter up the house with all of *their* collections. One son has a miniature National Jewish Archives. He uses every drawer, shelf and box he can find to house this vast collection. He has amassed ten years of historical material on religious, political, nationalistic, and military issues in Israel, including all relevant newspaper articles, posters, flyers, brochures, mailings, letters, notices and advertisements. His collection will undoubtedly be of great value someday. I just warned him that when the time comes, his future *kallah* can't have him without the collection. It's groom and papers or nothing at all.

My father *z"l*, was a man of action who didn't believe in saving junk, and while in the process of moving, he gave away a box of my favorite books by mistake. (He assumed that I had read them all and therefore didn't need them anymore. Otherwise, why were they packed separately from everything else?) To this day I remember each and every book in that box: Bambi and Bambi's Children; The Five Little Peppers and How They Grew; Heidi and Heidi's Children; Hans Brinker and the Silver Skates; and a book called Your Favorite Dog Stories. Years later, I replaced them all — except for the dog stories. And ever since, I unashamedly buy myself gifts of children's books whenever the spirit moves me.

I have found that marvelous old books surface in the most unexpected places, such as the old, ill-furnished apartment in Tzefat, where we somehow found ourselves during a few days of vacation. I discovered an entire dusty, mildewed array of classics, travel books, and other intriguing tidbits which no one had touched for long years past. I was then left with an agonizing decision: stay home and read or get on with the touring!

Reading habits vary as much as individuals. I tend to read during breakfast or in bed at night. And when I find something really good, I just drop everything else for a day or two and read straight through. These are the days the kids know they have to forage for themselves. Having accumulated a lot of foraging experience, they fare quite well.

My husband, on the other hand, has a reading problem. An ardent lover of *sefarim,* he collects them faster than he can learn them, which is a source of great frustration. I try to comfort him by pointing out that it's hard to just zip through something like the *Rambam* while having breakfast. But unless he switches over to easier, quicker reading, I have no solution to offer him.

He also tends to underline and write comments in the margins of books, which upsets me. I find that it breaks the flow of things, and my eyes jump ahead to the marked sections even though I tell them not to. After much deliberation, we compromised. He agreed to mark only his own books, and to read mine without a pencil or pen in hand.

I cannot end a chapter on books without mentioning my library card. The first one I ever got was an old-fashioned, yellow, lined card on which the librarian stamped the date you took out your books and the date you returned them. Those were the days when late returns meant a fine of two cents per book per day, and I was careful never to commit as flagrant a crime as returning late.

Like a piece of flat, yellow gold, that library card was precious to me. It opened up doors, and gave access to places far away, people one could never have met, and ideas and dreams to spin and weave into a new reality.

Today, like everything else, libraries aren't what they used to be. Library cards are uniform, magnetic, plasticized, and automatic. More important, tastes and morals have changed, and discerning parents are hard put to find suitable reading material for their children. Nonetheless, the magic of a really good book is still ours for the reading, and at the end of any day in our house, you can hear the plaintive cry echoing in and around our book-lined rooms and corridors: "Isn't there anything to read around here?"

# The Saga of a Dresser Drawer

he other day, in a moment of great moral weakness, I looked at a drawer. My husband's top dresser drawer, to be exact. Actually, it is not a drawer in the accepted sense of the word. It is more like a combined national museum, the family archives, our banking establishment, and a branch of the main Jerusalem *genizah*. Over the years, the dresser has drooped several inches as the aforesaid drawer has weighed heavily upon its lower sections.

Each Pesach, I patiently rearrange everything inside as neatly as possible, being careful not to throw anything out, waiting for my husband to make order. Who knows what irreplaceable treasures lie waiting here? Ancient wills and testaments? Forgotten checks? Kosher *mezuzos*? Priceless lottery tickets we never cashed in? A missing screw (perhaps the one the phonograph has been patiently awaiting for the past three years)? And keys — so many keys! Whenever did we have so many doors, locks, cases, bicycles, or cars needing such a vast collection of keys? Not a single one looked even vaguely familiar.

In short, I was facing a virtual Fort Knox of a drawer — neat, compressed, compacted and closed.

As I was saying, while trying to find something, and in a moment of weakness, I decided to make a little room. Women are not wily without reason, and I too have developed certain vital strategies for domestic survival throughout the years. In this particular case, I simply lifted two large shoe boxes of bank records out of the offending drawer — touching naught, disturbing nothing. I gently laid the boxes on top of the dresser. Now, with the boxes staring him in the face instead of being neatly tucked away in his drawer, my life-partner would have no choice but to go through them, discarding the chaff, making order, filing away paid bills and receipts.

Presto! I now had half an empty drawer, ready and waiting! I immediately began to fill it with important items which *belong* in a top dresser drawer, things like handkerchiefs and tie-clips, things which had been placed, helter-skelter, in other places because the dresser drawer was always filled to capacity. But once I started collecting these crucial objects from other drawers to place them in their proper resting place, I discovered that three additional drawers were now in a state of disarray, and in the process of setting things straight, I was left holding the bag.

Rather, a bag. A large plastic bag full of used *tzitzis*, vintage 1972-1987. Beautiful woolen *tzitzis*, long turned a warm golden yellow, and hung with parts of knots and strings and threads in a large array of sizes and shapes. I was actually holding a miniature family history of the *mitzvah* of *tzitzis!*

I gathered them all up lovingly, together with three pairs of old but still sturdy men's pajamas and six identical men's sweaters in varying shades of tan and gray and marched in on my husband.

"This all has to go out!" I announced firmly.

"O.K. I'll look at it tomorrow," came a mumble from behind a *gemara.*

"There's nothing to look at. The *tzitzis* are all *pasul;* the pajamas are ugly; the sweaters are falling apart; and I need the room."

"One sweater is for around the house; one's for around the neighborhood; one's for *Shabbos* and one's new."

"Three years is new?" I asked. "And the pajamas are older than that."

"I can wear the pajamas on top of my clothes the next time I paint the house."

"Since when do you paint the house? And in pajamas yet??"

"Leave the *tzitzis* here. I'll bring them to the *genizah* on *Rosh Chodesh.* "

"You need a New Moon to go to the *genizah*?" I asked incredulously.

"No," came the reply. "That's when the *genizah* is open."

I sighed and deposited the *tzitzis* bag on his table. At least one item was out of the bedroom. But my work was just beginning. Seeing as how the room was in such disarray, I threw all caution to the winds and opened up my own drawers.

The box of old cosmetics and jewelry I save for Purim was dumped, and a more current batch was put away for the holiday festivities. Newer purchases, stashed away until now in other parts of the house, finally made their way into my drawers. In the process, I found an expensive bottle of perfume I thought I had thrown out by mistake. (These are the little perks that keep you going in difficult jobs like these.) I also came across an entire package of old but unused out-of-style stockings and while trying to figure out what to do with them, my daughter walked in and asked excitedly, "Where did you get those? It's exactly what everyone is wearing now!" I hurriedly pushed them into her hand with instructions to put them in her drawer and wear them all by *Shabbos* before the style changes again.

Two and one half hours and four jingling wastebaskets full of garbage and keys later, I sat back and beamed at my gleaming dressers — five large, lovely, neatly arranged men's drawers and nine small, lovely, almost neatly arranged (I have more things than my husband does) women's drawers. I had really intended to relax and read a book that evening and here I was, exhausted, but it was worth it. (Certain pastimes tend to tire a person, but I'd rather be tired from having done something pleasurable, even if it's work, than from something I didn't enjoy!)

"You're still in the drawers?" asked my husband when he walked in and saw me cooing at the fourteen spiffy drawers. "I thought you went to sleep hours ago." Go explain the joys of cleaning to a man.

The following morning, my husband was limping. "What's wrong with your foot?" I asked.

"It's because of your cleaning," he complained.

"My cleaning?" I asked in confusion.

"Yes. You know, my top drawer."

"Your top drawer? What does the drawer have to do with the foot?"

"It has a lot to do with it!" he answered. "I opened the drawer to look for my car keys. By the way, all the keys disappeared. Did you see them anywhere? Anyway, I always open that drawer with a hard yank because it's so full and heavy. Now that you cleaned it, it's empty and light, and the whole thing flew right out onto my foot. Where did the keys go? I need the car to drive to *minyan*. And my foot is killing me!"

So much for appreciation. And by the way, the two large shoe boxes of bank records are still sitting on top of the dresser.

# No News is Good News

ur family represents a wide spectrum of well-formed opinions. We go from left to right, up to down, with lots of sideways in between. Independent thinkers all, our views are varied and vocal, and our table is the seat of much lively conversation.

The amazing thing is that despite the energy we expend on expounding, and despite the vast number of brain cells we each enlist in attempting to influence and persuade, only rarely does anyone succeed in convincing anyone else of anything at all. It's not that we're prejudiced or stubborn or unthinking; it's just that everyone is so wonderfully positive of the truth and justice of his own particular position. And good Jews that we are, and living as we do in Israel (that effervescent nerve-center of the universe), we are blessed with marvelously much to discuss and disagree on.

Nonetheless, the U.N. could learn a few things from us. Although our opinions and attitudes are far from unanimous, we have all managed to remain loving, good friends — tolerant and respectful of the other fellow's position — even when it isn't our own. Which is more than can be said about our attitude towards the media.

We listen to the news very vocally and we give as good as we get. The media in Israel are not known for their objectivity or their sympathy towards issues we consider to be important. But we have our revenge. Not a newscaster gets through our airspace without taking a bad beating on the way. For every sentence or announcement made, someone in the house has two or three ready in reply. And reply we do. Sometimes en masse, walking in and out of the kitchen, tossing out funny, cynical, cryptic or wise observations in the direction of the radio. If the family feedback gets too lively, it is periodically punctuated by a "Keep quiet for a minute! I can't hear what he's saying!" Which immediately produces a new crop of remarks. (I am of the opinion that *Kol Yisrael* should broadcast *our* news commentary. I have a sneaking suspicion that it might very well represent the *real* Voice of Israel.)

I always mean to write these pithy comments and commentaries down and send them to some newspaper, but I never do. If I did, I might get the country into better working order, but I'd never get the dishes done or the laundry folded, and some things are just more important than others. So the nation is left to muddle along as best it can, while our familial pearls of wisdom are lost to mankind. Such is the way of the world.

Newspapers are another aggravating topic. In recent years, my newspaper reading has decreased to a minimum, usually only once a week. Otherwise, I find that my days get tarnished by the pessimism and general malaise which is engendered by the press. The media manages to take the shine and polish off every bright new day, and I resent it. My days are a gift from *Hakadosh Baruch Hu* and they are nowhere nearby as bad and ugly and calamity-stricken as the editors would have me believe. G-d doesn't give rotten gifts.

I once read a story about some children who published a newspaper which contained only good, cheerful news. They were so successful that they eventually put the local paper out of business. I find that an intriguing and stimulating idea, one I am definitely considering for some future reincarnation.

One might sum up the news (from all countries, all stations, all satellites, all over the world) as: A lot of people making a living by having lots to say, most of which isn't worth saying, and the rest of it not adding up to all that much once it's been said. (Which does seem a rather wordy description, but considering what I'm dealing with, it's the best I can do.)

❧ ❧ ❧

I like to start my mornings with some non-verbal, fully orchestrated piece of classical music. Good music provides a relaxing background while I figure out how to begin the day (I get into work slowly in the mornings). Needless to say I never read the paper in the morning, even if we happen to have a current one around. Coffee and the news is not my idea of a good beginning.

Or one can listen to a tape. Singing alone isn't bad either, or humming. Even talking to one's self can be beneficial. It helps you think. And since most people find themselves to be agreeable, intelligent company, a personal, private conversation can save a lot of time and energy which might have been spent arguing with someone else.

My daughter has asked me not to indulge in these private (or idiosyncratic, as she politely refers to them) conversations when outsiders are in the house. But on the whole, I have found them to be a reasonably pleasant way of filling my mind without the help of the media. Try it sometime and see.

# Here and Now

## The Contemporary Scene

*These are the times that try men's souls. Yes, indeed, they surely are. Nor are they so easy on women. But, then again, which times are? Whatever time we find ourselves in, it always seems to be a difficult one, full of serious challenges, fraught with danger, and riddled with maddening inconsistencies. And we are, each and every one of us, enmeshed in the web of our times. Try as we may, there's no way to completely escape the influences and pressures which define, form and limit the age we live in.*

*Still, we do try. And if we can't always buck the values, the style or the system of our own era (it's always easier to evaluate someone else's), we can at least sit back, take a long look, and poke a few well-placed holes into the fabric of our Here and Now. And while we're at it, we can have a good laugh — not least of all, at ourselves.*

# The Electronic Age

lease understand. I'm the kind of person who used the same broom for twenty-two years, and every time someone asked, "Why don't you get a new one?", my standard answer was: "What's wrong with this one?" It took me seven years to discover a different and better kind of can opener; we're the only family I know that still boasts an 8mm movie camera; and when a toaster oven finally entered our home, everyone else was using a microwave. When it comes to new gadgets, there's no doubt that we're slow on the uptake. So when I went to America for a visit some time ago — the first such visit after seven or eight years — I was in for a few surprises.

Everyone knows that Americans are a busy bunch, always inventing something new and better to enhance the consumer's life-style (and to deflate his bank account). Nor had they been idle during my long absence. Nonetheless — and despite the fact that Israelis are a pretty gadget-conscious gang themselves — I was thoroughly unprepared for the advent of the Electronic Age. Take, for example, the case of the simple button.

When I was a kid, a button was what you used to close your coat or sweater. Sort of a cousin to the zipper. On occasion, a button-like object would be used for something else — like ringing a doorbell or turning on a machine. But suddenly, the button was no longer an accessory to apparel; it was the key to the new, electronic world.

In order to enter or leave my cousin's home, an entire array of buttons had to be pushed in proper sequence — and within the stipulated thirty seconds — or an ear-shattering alarm would go off and the police would arrive en masse. Everytime I left or entered the house by myself, I was a bundle of nerves. And indeed, I did once punch the wrong number. Within a minute, I found myself answering the phone, apologizing and explaining to the security system that I was just a confused cousin from Israel who didn't know how to properly work the alarm.

Closed as they were with their own protective devices, the windows also presented a problem to the uninitiated. So I sat in front of the hermetically shut panes, gazing out at the lovely fresh air and wondering what it smelled like. I was eventually told that it was unnecessary to open windows in American homes because the total air-conditioning system provided constant, clean, fresh air, while real fresh air only made everything dusty.

(Perhaps I should mention that in Israel, we open the windows to "air out the house" every day, all year long. Even during the cold winter. It's considered a healthy, housewifely thing to do. We also "air out" our rugs, mattresses, bedding and children.)

Then there were the fancy new telephones which, instead of

having ten faithful buttons, one for each number, now sported a good twenty or thirty, each with its own complex electronic system. The only person I could contact unaided was the Operator.

Even the faucets were problematic. In an elegant restroom in one of the finer department stores in the city, I stood in front of the sink for five entire minutes trying to figure out how to wash my hands. There was a faucet over the modern, streamlined sink, but no way of extracting any water. I bent down under the sink to check for possibilities, pretending I had dropped something on the floor. Nothing there. I felt the wall, thinking perhaps there was some sort of hidden panel or switch. I considered banging the fixture, much as Moshe had hit the rock. Finally, just as I was about to give up, I moved slightly, and in so doing, I put myself in front of an invisible electric eye. Presto! The water shot forth in full stream!

If I sound slightly behind the times, all I can say in my defense is, at the time of my visit, these marvels had not yet reached the Hamashbir Latzarchon department store in Jerusalem.

❀ ❀ ❀

One of the most American of America's playthings is, of course, the automobile. And a trip in a friend's recent purchase was a ride to remember. An automatic master key opened all the car doors at once, allowing us to slide down into a soft, plushy pilot's cockpit. (At least that's what the dashboard looked like to me.) But as I examined the intriguing array of buttons before me, I was almost knocked on the head by the buckle of a smoothly sliding seat belt which descended and enveloped me in a safety-net, extending from the shoulders to the thighs. For a moment, I was a bit taken aback, but my hostess assured me that I was not under attack. This was standard procedure.

We each chose our individualized air conditioning pro-

grams, set them at the proper height, direction and tempera-
ture (warmer for the legs, cooler for the face and shoulders)
and I sat back, prepared to experience the ultimate in earthly
transportation. I tried to open my window (I like the feel of the
wind in my face and air conditioning just isn't the same
thing), but in a repeat performance of the faucet, there was no
knob or switch available. When I sighed and made mention of
the lack of fresh air in the United States, my hostess
immediately pushed another magic button which raised and
lowered the windows, all four of them at once, until I was
sufficiently resuscitated.

The little Japanese lady who lives somewhere in my
friend's car-computer then announced in her funny voice that
if we would only lock the doors, turn on the motor and
arrange the mirror so that the car's electronic eye and the
driver's were in focus, we could take off. Push, punch, touch
on a few more buttons and we were on our way, driving
smoothly along on the automatic Cruise Control, free to
enjoy the freshly-conditioned air and the magnificent scenery
through the natural-looking tinted windows (blue trees began
to look normal after a while).

The only thing the car didn't supply was *Tefillas Haderech* -
the Traveler's Prayer. I guess the Japanese lady in the
computer never learned Hebrew.

❦   ❦   ❦

The most creative piece of electronics that we came across,
however, was in a stationery store. It was a little pocket-purse
flashlight - with no button to turn it on, of course. My sister
and I played with it for fifteen minutes, trying to figure out
how it worked. We finally turned to the instructions and were
told to "Chant and clap your hands to the rhythm of One
Potato, Two Potato, Three Potato, Four." We did, and miracle
of all miracles, that little flashlight knew exactly what to do. In
a mini-replay of *Vayehi Or*... "Let there be light" — it turned

itself on! Astounded, I could only gasp, "But what's it for?"

My sister (who by now was hysterical) could only gasp back between bouts of laughter. "It's for (ha ha). . .the dark, you know. . .at night (chuckle). . .when you can't find your keys in your (gasp) purse. So you do this clapping bit and the light turns on so you can see them (HA HA HA!)." At this point she absolutely fell apart, and, infected by her contagious laughter, I fell apart with her.

When a saleswoman came by to ask us if anything was wrong, we made a hasty exit, only to discover that we had walked out holding the Magic Lantern. For a moment I considered purchasing the thing, just to show them back home that it really existed, but I decided against it. If the neighbors heard clapping and strange chanting at some late hour in the darkened hall of our building, they might decide it was a case for the police. So back it went to the store. But the memory of that little light will continue to shine in my heart as a piece of Americana Deluxe.

# The Good Life

ombarded as we are with incessant advertising and unending Madison Avenue messages, we can't help but get hooked (some more, some less) on the Good Jewish Life so graciously offered to us on the pages of our Jewish press.

Multitudinous ads wedge their way into our brains, where they sit (taking up space which could be used by other, more valuable thoughts), winking coyly and constantly fighting for our attention. Like barnacles on a boat, they stick. I have discovered barnacles that inform us that:

1. *Today's kiddies must wear designer clothing.* The very latest. "The very latest" used to mean the newest hand-me-downs from an older cousin. We were glad to get them, too. And if necessary, they were indeed custom re-designed to fit the new owner.

2. *European Men's Fashions — Debonair, with Continental Flavor* — are on the market. Somehow, that brings to mind the kind of clothing that most immigrants tried hard to get away from. The American Look was in style then. Who wanted to look European? And "debonair"? Webster defines the word as "easy and carefree in manner; jaunty; sprightly; elegant; gracious; urbane." It all sounds intriguing, but except for the "gracious," what does it have to do with raising good Jewish boys?

One fancy firm is offering a *Unique Blend* — i.e., a combination of their clothes and You, the well-dressed male. "You" is depicted as a glamorous but cold, hard-looking character, sort of like a well dressed movie star turned yeshivah man. Some "blend"! Sounds like *shatnez* to me.

*Distinctive Elegance* in men's clothing is also "in," but my menfolk aren't playing that game either. *Distinctive Elegance* just doesn't seem to be their style. Which is just fine with me. It probably has to be dry-cleaned anyway.

3. *Women are entitled to Fashion,* although the High Style in which it's offered is not everyone's cup of tea.

*Custom Designed Couture for Every Occasion* sounds tempting, but is the kitchen an "occasion"? I wonder. The car pool? Somehow, even for *Shabbos*, Custom Designed Couture seems a bit much to handle. Of course, I suppose I'll never be a *Fashion Leader With a Tradition of Elegance in Ultra-Elegant Surroundings* (the laundry room?). Oh, well, I do the best I can.

I even mentioned to my husband that perhaps the time has come to begin our *Collection to Mark Significant Moments.* Until now, all I've collected are funny greeting cards, books, and some records. A few diamond tiaras, brooches, and bracelets, the kind that marked Significant Moments in the ad, would be a nice change.

I will not, however, under any circumstances, contemplate punk. That is to say, *Hairstyles for Today's Woman.* If G-d wanted Today's Woman to be hideous and ugly, he would have made her that way to begin with.

4. And there is the Home — the Jewish Home — that bastion, castle, the very forge of the Jewish people. Now if you're going to forge, you may as well do it in style, and the ads are all there to help you.

*Turn Your Boudoir into a Haven of Ultimate Luxury.* Well, I would, really I would. Except that I don't have one. A boudoir, that is. All I have is a bedroom, and I often use the beds for folding laundry.

My *Key to Success — A Suite of Elegant Office Furniture* consists of a kitchen table, a *shtender* (which takes the overflow from the table) and whichever chair is closest.

Unfortunately, we don't own a *Secluded Oceanfront Villa on a Tropical Island — For Religious.* Unless a Centrally Located Apartment (Condominium?) in a Religious Area in the Middle East qualifies. Our Centrally Located doesn't possess a *Multi-Station Home Gym* or *A Total Concept in Interior Design,* but it does have a nice, homey feel to it, and we are grateful.

Our *Ultimate in Fine Furniture* will have to wait for a fire-sale, but we did purchase an antique-looking three-legged stool for our telephone corner which matches the rocking chair (by now nearly antique) we bought when our first son was born. When we bought the rocker, my father wanted to know who was still selling such *alte shmattes.* I reassured him that President Kennedy was using one, but he didn't really believe me. Everyone knew that Kennedy could afford something more modern than that! Today, I like to think of our rocker and matching telephone stool as our very own *Piéces de Résistance* — my own personal resistance to the kind of pieces the stores out there are trying to sell me!

The one thing I can't quite grasp in the Home Furnishings Field is the fixation on fixtures. *50,000 Feet of Bathroom Fixtures On Display!* So crieth one ad. Foot by foot, every inch can be seen at a local fixture company. It's an awful lot of bathroom to look at.

5. Food is a world unto itself. Now that there are twenty (thirty? forty? fifty?) thousand products with a *hechsher* on them, we can eat our way into Eternity. *Tantalizing Tastes, Sumptuous Menus, Pleasurable Memories — all in Luxurious Surroundings to Pamper You.*

My most tantalizing tastes, menus and memories are from my bubby's *Sedarim,* although I don't remember much about the luxurious surroundings. They seem to have been rather noisy and crowded, but no one minded. And we were definitely pampered, even if we weren't Pampered. (Disposable diapers weren't even a distant dream in those days.)

The most interesting food ad I ever came across was about chocolate "moldings." What, I wondered, is a chocolate molding? I had visions of ceiling moldings bordering a room in dark, rich, melty chocolate and slowly dripping down the walls. Bring out the ladders and climb up for a lick!

*Are You Still Drinking Ordinary Wine?* asks one ad. No, I answer. I drink *Shabbos* Wine. That makes it Extraordinary, don't you think?

Well, then, how about a night out? *The Road to Kosher Heaven* is lined with glatt-kosher pizzerias, *mehadrin* hamburger joints, sixty-five deliciously *hechshered* ice cream flavors (remember when they just had chocolate and vanilla?), and in Israel, *Glatt Al Ha'eish* (which is Hebrew for Barbecued Glatt).

And, so they tell us, the *Epicurean Redemption is Finally Here.* Not only on Pesach, but all year round. If you aren't already eating in a restaurant several times a week, you should, at the very least, be frequenting your nearest Take-Out, Take-Home Place. From kishke to *katchke,* if it's edible, someone is selling it — koshered, cooked, ready and waiting.

*We have taken care of All Your Shalach Manos Needs!*

shouts one paper; *Shabbos Comes Ready Made!* cries another. *Floating Sedarim* are now being celebrated all over the Caribbean; and on Rosh Hashanah, make your reservations and, like Avraham Avinu, head straight to Rosh Hahar — the mountains.

❦ ❦ ❦

Dripping with adjectives, the ads read like a thesaurus. Exquisite, incomparable, elegant; sparkling, sophisticated, superb. Privileged, pleasurable, stunning. Extraordinary, ultra, infinite and beyond. The Horn of Plenty is overflowing, and its pleasures and possessions are ours for the taking (i.e., paying). A fitting motto might be: Have checkbook; will travel . . . or buy, or eat, or decorate. The *Ultimate Experience, Life-Style, Look,* is there and waiting.

If the going gets a bit expensive, there is always the *Friendly Funding Corporation Which Offers a Wide Range of Loans.* And while facing the music, we can hire the band which plays *Music to Match the Moment. . .*

❦ ❦ ❦

Personally, I like a plain, old-fashioned ad that says what it has to say in plain, old-fashioned words. Words that mean something, as in *Remnant Sale - Good Buy For Your Money.* Then I can decide — all by myself — if the product is Elegant or Exquisite enough to turn my home or my family or myself into an Ultimate Design.

It seems to me that most people are pretty Ultimate as is. We come in millions of distinct styles and designs, each one a unique blend, uniquely crafted. And if we could only shed some of our Madison Avenue barnacles, maybe we'd be freer to enjoy the Good Lives we already possess.

# Es a Bissel:
# The Cooking Connection

"**D**on't talk while you eat." Generation after generation has been drilled with that simple maxim. Yet there seems to be some universal connection between speaking and eating that keeps the two together despite all the educating to the contrary. Like two good friends, food and speech march hand in hand (or mouth and mouth) down the table of history.

Food and its preparation are an eternal human concern, a consuming human activity, and an endless topic of human conversation. Since the beginning of time, people have been eating — and talking about it. The very first sin committed involved a discussion and then a bite. (Just imagine, had Chavah only refused to speak to the snake, the entire story might have ended differently!) But even though that first eating spree brought death to the world, food is inextricably bound up with life and love. The lovely Yiddish adage says it all: *Es a bissel, mein kind* — Eat a little, my child.

Food, however, is not only love and kisses. It is hard work too. *Gan Eden* was the ultimate in instant eating, and part of the punishment visited upon Adam and Chavah was the need to cook and prepare their food. But *Hashem's* "punishments" are not vindictive. They are meant to comfort and console and heal.

So Chavah and her descendants took to cooking with a vengeance; a vengeance spiced with love, sprinkled with creativity, and baked, broiled or roasted to satisfaction.

An interesting culinary observation is the fact that more books about food and cooking are published per year than books on any other topic. No matter how many gourmet cookbooks come out, there is always one more around the corner, including kosher ones. Kosher Chinese, Jewish Japanese, Sephardi Indian; *mehudar* low-calorie snacks; no-cholesterol *yom tov* brunches; fatless, high-protein *simchah* dinners; *milchig* party menus; *fleishig* holiday feasts, and *pareve* tea-time tidbits. There is seemingly no end to our interest in what we eat and how we prepare it. Why is this so, when we actually require very little to stay alive and well?

And whenever people get together, the chances are good that somewhere in the room, a conversation will develop on the subject of food: restaurants, recipes, food-related problems and illnesses, children's feeding problems, the high price of food, or the supermarket or butcher or baker with the best bargains.

While eating to stay alive may be the original goal, our concerns with food far surpass pure biological necessity. Otherwise, how can one explain our constant involvement with what we eat? After all, basic food preparation is not all that difficult, especially today when few of us have been subjected to plucking chickens, hand-churning butter, or producing other staples of the not-too-distant past. And we could conceivably eat the same menu day in day out (as people often did, and in many places, still do) and be perfectly well-fed and healthy (probably more so than we are now).

There are surely deep secrets awaiting discovery here, but one thing is certain. Food is much more than fuel for our bodies. Eating is also a way of hallowing our bodies and the produce of the world around us; of fueling our psyche; of providing love and security; a form of *chessed* and a great social bash. And because it serves all these functions, it offers unending opportunities for that creative activity commonly referred to as cooking.

❦ ❦ ❦

Take the lowly chocolate chip cookie, an unattractive clump of brownish dough if ever there was one. Yet except for a few unrepentant misanthropes, who can help but drool at the mere mention of this commodity? And of course the chocolate chip cookies *my* mother used to make were absolutely unbeatable. No matter that your mom made them too, together with a million other moms, all using the exact same recipe found on the back of the chocolate chip bag. *My* mom's were different. Because, if you haven't guessed by now, *my* mom's cookies came with a special ingredient — her own brand of mother-love, just for me. Your mom only gave me some of the cookies she had baked for you. And you'd be amazed at what a difference the secret ingredient of love can make in a cookie.

My father, for example, always insisted that his mother's challah and cakes were tastier than my mother's, even though my mother's (she was a superb gourmet cook and baker) were actually far superior. But in the taste bud scheme, reality often takes second place to fond childhood memories.

One of my own childhood memories is my father announcing (usually at mealtimes): When hunger comes in the door, love flies out the window! In my mind's eye I see Hunger — a tall, humped, skinny, and menacing visitor — coming through the kitchen door, while Love — small, pinkish, chubby (undoubtedly well fed) and heartshaped — hurriedly flies out the window so as not to be demolished by the evil, uninvited guest.

🦋  🦋  🦋

But even more important than taste buds is the topic of immortality, for believe it or not, that is often the reward for sharing food via a recipe. Note the following story. It might be called "The Enduring Saga of a Pizza."

We have a recipe for pizza in our house which is duly recorded in our somewhat grimy, well-used cookbook as "Esty's Pizza." Why Esty? Because my daughter got the recipe from her friend Esty. One day, however, when I mentioned something to Esty's mother about Esty's Pizza, her mother looked puzzled and said "Oh, you mean Beyla's Pizza?"

"Who's Beyla?" I asked.

"She's the one who gave Esty the pizza recipe Esty gave Shani. I think it's called Chana's Pizza in Beyla's house because Beyla got it from her cousin Chana."

Intrigued with this information, I made a few phone calls to some of Shani's friends and discovered, to my delight, that Esty's (Beyla's-Chana's) Pizza had successively evolved from Shani's Pizza to Miri's Pizza and Someone Else's Pizza (I lost track by then). How wonderful, I thought to myself, to be so lovingly inscribed as a link in the chain in the Book of Pizza!

Actually, I shouldn't have been surprised. Sometime after my mother z"l passed away, my sister and I were going through her many cookbooks. They read like a history of her long and rich social life. "Leah's rogelach"; "Shirley's French pastry"; "Betty's fish"; "Hanna's meatballs"; "Edith's kneid-lach"; and on and on and on. It was like a culinary replay of the many people she had met and loved. And it was comforting to think that in scores of homes across the world, hundreds of mouth-watering recipes which she passed on are duly recorded ... "Dorothy's Carrot Kugel"; "Dorothy's Nut-Tuna Casserole"; "Dorothy's Turkey Stuffing and Sauce," ad infinitum. (In fact, my own feelings about my mother's recipes are so strong that whenever I pass them on, I always insist that they be written down as Yaffa's Mother's Recipes, and not as my own.)

My own favorite recipe book is *The I-Hate-to-Cookbook* by Peg Bracken. I acquired this little treasure through the good graces of my friend Rachel, the world's most vicarious cook. Rachel loves food, both the thinking about and the eating of, but not the preparing for. She collects cookbooks — lovely, gastronomical, eye-appealing, mouth-watering books with beautiful, full-color photographs. You can almost taste them.

She had picked up *The I-Hate-to-Cookbook* on her way out of a bookstore, but once home, had realized it was not up to her gourmet standards. Rather apologetically, she gave it to me. "I bought it by mistake," she said. "Maybe you'll like it." I did. It was my league par excellence.

A skinny black and white paperback, *The I-Hate-to-Cook-book* was full of Peg Bracken's funny prose and her marvel-ously simple, serviceable, quick and easy-to-make recipes. Just the kind of thing I'd always dreamed about. I have since cooked the book to an early death. It is spattered and spotted beyond reading and is held together with a *milchig* rubber band.

❀ ❀ ❀

"You are what you eat." Who hasn't heard these words of wisdom time and time again? Kosher animals help keep you *tahor* — pure; the fruits of *Eretz Yisrael* infuse you with a form of *kedushah*. But it works in the physical sense too, of course. Some foods make you healthy; others make you sick. One wonders what effect today's frozen and fried food climate will have on humanity. Will we all turn into identical icicles waiting to be warmed in some mass microwave oven? Will our complexions take on the hue of the many food colorings we ingest?

We have already removed cholesterol, calories, chemicals, fats, and flavors; sugars, salts, additives, and most nutrition from our food (which we then pump full of reinforced vitamins for added health). It is a sad commentary that the most generously fed generation in the history of mankind eats so poorly.

Yet Jewish respect for food remains axiomatic. We make a *brachah* on everything we eat, thereby sanctifying the raw material of our world and transforming those chocolate chips into a spiritual delight. (I'll bet you a cupcake that when David Hamelech legislated the compulsory hundred blessings per day to more or less cover the gamut of human activity, never in his wildest dreams imagined that we moderns could manage a hundred *brachos* a day just on our stomachs!)

I recently discovered that there is a *halachah* requiring us to look at our food while making a blessing — so that we think about it, appreciate it, and feel properly thankful. None of this mumble-jumble stuff under your breath, just to be *yotzei* so you can get on with the eating of it!

Our respect for food extends even to its demise, making us hesitate to throw away anything that's even vaguely edible. I will keep leftovers which I know for a fact no one will ever touch (let alone eat) in my refrigerator for days. I will keep them until they develop a fuzzy, greenish topping and can be safely thrown out. But Heaven forbid that I throw them away while they are still in their prime. The voice of my bubby, *z"l,* telling us about the poor starving children in Europe, is still distinct.

At every celebration I attend, I am uncomfortable when I see the waiters remove perfectly good food from the table, knowing that it will most likely find its final resting place in the municipal garbage dump. One very fine practice I came across was in Chicago, where people donate leftover food from weddings and bar mitzvahs to a local Jewish welfare organization which repacks it and sends it to people in need.

❋ ❋ ❋

And so the story of food continues down through the generations with no end in sight. Children grow up, marry and move out. Styles in clothing change. Pets and plants die and are replaced. People leave jobs, sell their homes, move to different neighborhoods or cities, and make new friends. But Food and the Cooking Connection are with us forever.

# Instant Communication

ur house has no doorbell. Actually, there is a doorbell, but it's disconnected. Once, during a particularly busy Purim *seudah*, we discovered that we couldn't eat. Everytime we picked up a fork, the bell rang, literally bringing the world to our doorstep. *Shalach manos*, donations, people who were passing by and stopped in to say hello, and just bell-ringers who felt they were adding to the jubilant holiday spirit — all left their prints on the small, round button opposite our *mezuzah*.

After the appetizer and soup turned refrigerator cold and the doorbell rang for the thirty-second time in thirty-two minutes, we decided to disconnect it for half-an-hour in order to finish our meal before it congealed into solid ice.

The half hour has lasted for fifteen relatively peaceful, ringless years. (People coming to our door knock.) During this time, however, most other semblances of peace and quiet in our busy lives have long since disappeared. Like everyone else, we are caught up in a wave of electronic communications which seems to have engulfed the solar system.

Not long ago, I went into a small appliance store to purchase a telephone.

"What kind?" asked the salesgirl.

"Wall phone," I answered. "With buttons. The kind you punch, not dial."

"What kind?" she asked again.

"I just told you — wall phone, touch-dial."

"What kind?" came the unchanging reply.

I look around the display counter. "Yellow."

"What kind?"

"What do you mean 'what kind'? I told you what kind!" My voice rose slightly.

"Lady," she said while filing her nails, "there are phones for AT&T, for TT&A, and AA&T. There are phones with automatic redial and standard phones. There are phones with manual mute buttons, automatic muting, and hearing aid compatibility. All come with or without off-ringer switches."

She stopped to catch her breath and then went on.

"You can have a phone with alternate long distance services and a clock radio, or a hands-free phone with modular or regular plugs and illuminated dial pads. All models come with or without battery backups."

"Battery backups?" I mumbled.

"Oh, yeah, I almost forgot. There's tone-pulse switchable, with both pulse and rotary dialing, mountable or desk top models."

"Just a plain phone," I muttered feebly.

"Single line or double? Cordless? Ten memory numbers, twenty, forty? What kind of phone do you want, lady? What kind?"

At that point, I gave up. "I'll have to think about it," I

answered. And I have. My decision was to stick with my old green wall phone and take it off the hook whenever I want to take a nap undisturbed.

But then again, I'm not quite into electronic conversations. I like to speak to one human being at a time, uninterrupted, if possible. My friends have two or three lines, and their telephone conversations go something like this:

"Sarah? Hi! What's new? Really? Oh, just a minute. There's a call on the other line. . . Chani? How are the kids? I'm so glad you called. I'm anxious to discuss it with you. But can you wait a minute? I'm talking to Sarah on the other line." Ad infinitum.

And then there are the answering machines. Very well behaved too. If you don't mind a monologue, an answering machine can be a very satisfying form of communication. They're marvelous listeners who never interrupt. Just make sure you finish what you have to say before the final beep.

Which brings us to beepers. Even if you aren't sitting in your office or car, you can still stay in instant touch with the world via a beeper. But personally, I find beepers disconcerting. They're as bad as that double or triple line telephone, where it's all a person can do to finish a conversation uninterrupted. Persistent and demanding, the beeper alerts its wearer that he is wanted — somewhere, by someone else. And when the Master Beeper beeps, it expects to be answered!

The automobile, that last earthly bastion of privacy, is now routinely connected. No doubt the two line car-phone already exists as well. Somehow, a driver doing business on a car-phone gets my danger signals going. If it took three angels to deliver three messages to Avraham Avinu, how can one driver take so many and still wend his way safely through traffic? Perhaps divinely-sent angels in Avraham's time were only unitrack, while drivers with car-phones are multifaceted!

And wonder of all wonders. An air-phone is now on the market so you don't miss anything between cities in the sky. I wonder if this new wonder will make our prayers more audible to He Who Dwells On High (although I've always learned that if only we paid a little more attention to what we're saying, we already possess Direct Dialing to Him).

The communications explosion has led to some interesting connections. People nowadays have spoken to strangers in Switzerland, Haiti and Alaska — by mistake, of course — when they thought they were calling America, Israel and England. It's not a very direct form of communication, but it's a wonderful way of uniting our fragmented world, sort of a Universal Wrong Numbers Incorporated.

Instant information is also in. Dial one of thousands of toll-free numbers and everything you've always wanted to know but couldn't be bothered to learn is at your fingertips (and earlobes). Want to check the price of shoes in Montana? Model numbers for can-openers in Florida? Interest rates in Oshkosh? Discover your city, state, federal, and universal rights and wrongs, and what you can do about them? An "800" number will tell you all. Usually twenty-four hours a day, seven days a week. You can even Dial-a-Daf-Yomi (in several languages) and presto! Instant communication with Sinai!

And if this mind-boggling proliferation of the spoken word still isn't enough for you, for a few cents you can dispatch a few written words via telex, express mail or a fax machine, connected to your own private telephone and PC. One little modem provides instant, universal hook-up.

❀ ❀ ❀

Why do we have this compulsive need for instant communication? Why do we subject ourselves to this constant inundation of words and messages and information, even when it's not for business-related purposes? Would anything dreadful really happen if the answering machine didn't answer, the beeper didn't beep, and Chani called back tomorrow morning, when she could have her own private, personal conversation without waiting for Sarah to finish?

And must our kids have their own private telephone lines (preferably one per teenager)? Can't they be told to wait for the phone? And not to keep the line busy too long once they get through? You know — those old-fashioned concepts of sharing and consideration? Are all of our conversations really so terribly, terribly vital? We survive without them on *Shabbos* (a fact which non-observant Jews and gentiles cannot fathom), so a little abstention during the week can't be all that life-threatening.

Sometimes the world seems to be afflicted with ECF (Electronic Communications Fatigue). People are enervated, exhausted and nervous, and no wonder. Who wants to be plugged in twenty-four hours a day?

That's why our doorbell remains disconnected and our old green phone (no memory, no modem, no batteries) goes off the hook for naps. It's the only way to find a little peace and quiet.

# A Harried Existence

ARRIED. That described me. I suffered from a lack of time and a lack of mental leisure. I didn't mind being busy, but I couldn't stand always hurrying to finish Thing Number One because I had to start Thing Number Two. And when I reached Thing Number Two, I was already planning Thing Number Three. No matter what I was doing, my mind was always into the next job ahead. Between orthodontist appointments, broken washing machines, baking birthday cakes and bank balances, I felt like an overworked computer.

Although I found the time (somehow) to do almost everything, it was done in a state of constant turmoil. Sometimes, I wanted to just sit down, all alone in a corner, and quietly collapse. Even when I had a few minutes free, the wheels in my head continued to turn, round and round, full speed ahead. And what I didn't finish planning during the day was done at night. Even in my sleep, it was All Systems Go.

One day, in the midst of cleaning the shower head, the solution hit me like a lightning spray of clear, cold water. My children were still young. The work, the planning and organizing, the running around and the resulting complications would obviously not end in our house for a long time. And the things I was doing had to be done. My idea, therefore, was simple. Instead of walking around with a headache, I would faithfully write everything down on a Master List and then quit thinking about it!

If it was time to *daven*, I would *daven* with *kavanah* instead of flying through the pages so I could "start" the morning. If I was cleaning the living room, I'd concentrate on the vacuuming, not on my shopping. Shopping was down there on the List; its turn would come. And on my way to the supermarket, I'd concentrate on the traffic instead of cluttering up my mind with thoughts of supper.

Later in the day, while preparing supper, I'd do it with relish and enjoy the task of feeding my family. I wouldn't mull over getting the two youngest kids into bed early so I could sneak out on time to a P.T.A. meeting. And when bedding down those two little kids, I'd do it with all my heart. I would not skimp on the story or the tucking in or listening to their *Shema*. (Skimping invariably prolongs the procedure anyway.) If I couldn't finish the day's work before the evening, all I had to do was recopy the undone items onto the bottom (or top) of the next day's list.

What eventually happens when one is working with a list is that the really vital things (or the things one really wants to do) get done. The less important (or less appealing) items stay at the bottom of the list. Eventually, their turn comes too. Or better yet, sometimes they get so stale that they fall off the list altogether, thereby making room for some new item.

Sounds simple? Believe me, it's not. After years of trying, it's still difficult. Thinking of the task at hand, enjoying each moment as it comes instead of constantly living in the future and using the present only as a springboard — it takes discipline. But I try to stick with it. I want to feel that I am living in the Now, savoring and utilizing each day to its fullest. A floor washed should mean a clean floor whose shine makes me happy and hurray for the exercise that went with it. A phone call to a friend should be ten (twenty?) minutes of enjoyable communication without feeling guilty about wasting time. An hour spent waiting at the dentist should be an hour of rational planning (if I feel it's necessary) or else an hour of uncluttered relaxation reading a book.

I'm the first to admit that it doesn't always work. There are times when my mind starts wandering like a puppy off the leash, and I find myself planning next week or next month in advance, detail by detail. My thinking apparatus shifts into third gear and my brain begins to rush and race around. After all, without rushing, how can I possibly get everything done?

But I fight it. I lower my horizons and look down at one of my lists. I try to stick with today and do what has to be done now.

Because, after all, there is always only one today, and if we are forever spending our todays planning our tomorrows, when will we have time to get anything done?

# Writer's Cramp or
# How Not to Start a Career

 was going to be a writer. I had decided. After working on it for several years, I had a unique list of accomplishments to show for my efforts. To wit:

1. One book manuscript sent out, receipt of which was actually acknowledged. All I had to do was wait (and wait. . .and wait. . .) until someone at the publishing house read it.

2. One long article rejected by three well-known magazines.

3. Two articles written for a government office and actually printed. By some mysterious computer mistake, I was able to collect only 60% of the price agreed upon.

4. One children's story submitted to and gratefully accepted by a quality children's magazine. They forgot to make any mention of payment.

5. An absolutely charming book of children's poetry pronounced "unsalable in its present form."

6. A series of articles which a small magazine had been reprinting over and over for several years. It was heartening to keep seeing my name in print, but it got a little embarrassing when people started asking, "But didn't I see that article a few weeks (or months, or years) ago?"

There were, here and there, several items which were actually published and paid for, but they were the exception, not the rule. Just enough to give me a tantalizing mini-taste of success and to keep me going.

After pondering the situation, I decided that I was in need of some professional advice. I borrowed a friend's Writer's Guide vintage 1959. Assuming that things hadn't changed too much in seventeen years (it was 1976 at the time), I took the plunge and began to read. After only a few chapters, I made several important discoveries.

1. "Any story beginning with 'Once upon a time' is immediately suspect." Problem: I had just sent away a story beginning with 'Once upon a time. . .'

2. "Stick to your locale. If you live in N.Y., don't write about people living in Alabama or Alaska unless you have done painstaking research on these places!" Problem: I had lived in Chicago and Jerusalem. Two months earlier, I had written a children's story about a family in Alaska. My painstaking research had consisted of flipping through back issues of National Geographic.

3. "People who have had something published and are mentioned in a magazine or newspaper are inevitably inundated with letters and requests for inside tips, information and general words of wisdom and encouragement." The gist of this was, have pity on the poor souls and leave them

alone. They probably don't know much more than you do anyway. Problem: In my abysmal ignorance, I had just sent a letter to a writer whose name I saw in an article, asking about the books she had published, and if she had any general information on the subject for me.

I stayed up very late the night I read these pearls of wisdom, mulling over it all.

"If," I asked myself, "one commits all the expected blunders but reaps few of the hoped-for rewards, doesn't it seem silly to keep on with it? I could get some relaxing job selling women's hosiery and bring home a steady salary.

"Yes," I decided grimly. "It is silly. Silly and stupid and a waste of time. I shall put an end to it. But before I quit, I just want to sit down one last time and write this decision up!"

Wherein lies a major ingredient in most successful careers. Together with the hard work and the indispensable portion of divinely-administered *mazal,* it also helps to be obstinate, tenacious, persevering, stubborn and downright persistent.

One of my favorite "writer's stories" is about the wonderful book *Anne of Green Gables* by L.M. Montgomery. A children's novel (in the genre of *Little Women),* it was first published in 1910 after having been rejected by no less than fifteen publishers. The sixteenth struck it rich, and so did the author. Translated into thirty languages with more than eight million copies sold, *Anne* has touched the hearts of readers young and old around the globe. And she's still going strong.

And then there's the story about the forty-year-old woman who decided to write a book. Her family gave her a year's vacation from all housework and she sat in the library researching her novel. When she finally finished, it was rejected by no less than forty publishers. (She had sent it around according to an alphabetical list, and patient woman that she was, she just went down the list, one by one.)

It was accepted by the forty-first company. And became a

Book-of-the-Month Club selection. And a national best-seller. With, if I remember correctly, movie, paperback, and translation rights waiting to be sold for additional hefty sums.

All of which is what I'd call enlightening and encouraging. (I would probably have quit after the fifth rejection.) No matter which road we travel, it helps to practice those five unsung virtues. *Be obstinate; be tenacious; stick with it; persevere; and persist.* And one day, you may even see your name in print!

# There's No Place Like Home

## Life in Israel

*How does one go about introducing a topic which should need no introduction? Something as old as Creation, and as central to the Torah as all the other mitzvos combined?*

*Yet even today, in our small, highly connected world where criss-crossing the planet by jet is almost as common as a trip to the local supermarket, Eretz Yisrael still seems strange and faraway to many Jews. Even worse, its image is often warped and distorted; its reality neither properly understood nor appreciated.*

*As a nation, we have suffered hard and long because of that first mistaken evaluation of the Promised Land by the meraglim. It colored and affected our senses, our sense, and our experiences throughout Jewish history. The challenge of relating to the Land of Israel in the proper manner remains with us today.*

*But how can one relay and share that very special dimension of joy, of kedushah, of uniqueness which, despite all of the difficulties and the problems, is the heritage of those privileged to live in Israel today? The best way, of course, is to simply be here, and experience it first hand. The next best is to open the doors of one's heart and mind from afar. If we look and listen with love, understanding and appreciation will follow. For G-d enters a house when He is invited in. When the doors are closed, His Presence remains outside.*

*This section is about everyday life and living in the old dream/new reality of Israel . . . that section of the biblical* Eretz Yisrael *which our generation has been privileged to resettle. But perhaps it's really about opening doors, and minds, and hearts.*

# A Jewish Vocation

y the time I was eight or nine, I had already chosen my vocation. I was going to be a shepherdess, just like Avraham Avinu and Moshe Rabbeinu and David Hamelech. I even had my pasture staked out. It was a rather steep but nicely rounded hill, covered with grass and flowers and trees; with rolling mountains (or steep ones — depending on how I felt that day) in the background. It was, of course, in *Eretz Yisrael.*

The Land of Israel always seemed the proper place to be. I already knew what the *Kotel* and *Kever Rachel* and the *Me'arat Hamachpeyla* looked like from pictures on our *b'samim* box. I knew about Rebbi Meyer Baal Hanes in Teveria from his *pushke.* I was redeeming land for the Jewish people by putting money in the blue and white J.N.F. box. (In those days, many *balebatesha* Jewish homes had a J.N.F. box.) And I had laboriously purchased my very own trees, leaf by leaf. I paid ten cents a leaf, twenty leaves per tree, and the certificates with my name printed on them proved it.

I remember when we heard that the Jewish State had finally been declared. We were eating in the kitchen when the radio announced the long-awaited news. Time stood still for a moment as my parents — together with Jews around the world — laughed and cried and drank a *lechayim*. I didn't quite understand the significance of it all, but I did realize that something momentous had just occurred, something that seemed to be making *Eretz Yisrael* less of a dream and more of a reality. I was just a child, yet even older and wiser people did not foresee the crucial challenges this new reality would thrust upon the Jewish people, nor how long and hard we would have to work to meet them. But for a few moments, all worries were laid aside. We were happy, hopeful, and very thankful.

There weren't many people who traveled to Palestine (or even to Israel!) in those days. It was at least a twenty-four hour trip with five or six stops in propeller planes; it was expensive; and it was not terribly safe. When the grandparents of a schoolfriend planned a trip, intending to take my friend with them, I was thunderstruck. Someone my age who would actually set foot in *Eretz Yisrael!* It was hard to digest. And when she asked what I'd like her to bring back for me, the most obvious, logical thing was a piece of the Land itself — a bag of dirt. What could possibly be more precious than that?

To this day, we have our own private family custom. Whenever someone travels to *chutz la'Aretz* (that wonderfully-Jewish, amorphous designation for every place in the world that isn't part of the One Important Place), he or she takes a small stone along — a little piece of the Center of the Earth. It's sort of like taking along a picture of someone you love when you have to leave for a while. If *Chazal* could roll on the ground in the dust of *Eretz Yisrael,* I figure it can't be too crazy to add a small stone to the rest of my luggage. Sort of keeping the dream and the reality together.

❀ ❀ ❀

We grew up with them both, the dream and the reality. They were part and parcel of our home. The *pushkes*, the pictures, the prayers; the *meshulachim* and the few, special people who had actually been there. We had our collections of stamps, coins, and olivewood items, and we listened incessantly to the news. (My father *z"l* bought *The Daily Forward* — the Yiddish paper — for years, solely because it gave fuller, better coverage on Palestine than any of the English papers.) Like Rabbi Yehudah Halevi, we lived in the West, but our hearts and eyes and ears were always facing East.

Years later, my husband and I took a giant step forward into "reality." Together with our two small children, we left the large, beneficent United States amidst teary farewells, and made our way towards distant shores, much as our grandparents had done a generation or two before in the opposite direction. But they had merely come to a new resting place, another station in the Jews' long journey through the world, while we . . . we were finally going home.

A long time has passed since then. The two little ones we brought with us now have children of their own, all "local products" — new but legitimate shareholders in the country's real estate. As direct descendants of Avraham Avinu, they hold everlasting stock in "the company."

❀ ❀ ❀

As time went on, the old, classic pictures of my youth changed. The *Kotel* is now higher and wider, with space enough to hold tens of thousands of Jews — the result of a mammoth archaeological and renovation job begun immediately after the Six Day War. *Kever Rachel* is no longer a solitary dome in a field, but is hemmed in on all sides by the city of Beit Lechem. Jews once again live within walking distance of the *Me'arat Hamachpeyla* in Chevron. All are oft-visited places, a mere bus ride away from our home.

The J.N.F. forests, many of which were planted with "my" trees, are visible from our porch. And a large yeshivah full of lively youngsters graces the once lonely *kever* of Rebbi Meir Baal Hanes in Teveria.

The Jewish State has brought with it miraculous blessings, vexing problems, unanticipated challenges, and yes, even sorrows. Nonetheless, the dream still exists, and guided by the Hand of G-d, a new reality is taking shape. It will take time, and much effort, and many more tears until the work is completed. But that doesn't come as a surprise; we were warned long ago that *Eretz Yisrael,* like the Torah, is one of three vital gifts which are gained only through *yisurim* — through hardships.

❧   ❧   ❧

Meanwhile, we are grateful, and privileged, and humbled to be here. Who would ever have thought that we, or our parents, would *daven* before the *Kotel?* And just imagine — our children never even knew a Yerushalayim without the Old City! Or an *Eretz Yisrael* without Chevron, Yericho, Shechem and Beit El. They walk easily in the footsteps of their forefathers — in a Land promised to them long, long ago. Theirs is an unbelievable prophecy-come-true-reality we can scarcely comprehend, even today.

Perhaps those old day-dreams about shepherds and shepherdesses aren't so far out after all. Like the shepherds of old, our job is still to protect, to nourish, to guard. And our prototypes are still those famous shepherds — Avraham Avinu, the first to come; Moshe Rabbeinu, who so longed to come but was allowed to see the Land only from afar; and David Hamelech, a local lad, born and raised on holy soil in Beit Lechem, a mere half-hour from where we live. Gentle shepherd, fierce fighter, singer of psalms, and everlasting king, he filled the Land with the spirit and glory of G-d.

May it be our privilege to do the same.

# English It Ain't

nowledge of the English language is a valuable commodity in today's world, and most Americans who come on *aliyah* are anxious for their children to possess it. For many of us, English is also the only means of communication between our children and the families we left behind in the "old country."

But English-speaking parents in Israel face all sorts of strange and unexpected problems. As college-educated, second-generation Americans, it never occurred to us, even though we live in Israel, that our children might not speak English well. The world, however, is full of surprises, and this was one more to add to the list.

All things considered, we were relatively lucky. Although the English we heard from our kids was rather unusual, it was still a recognizable form of the language. Some Israeli children refuse to speak any English to their parents. (Just think back to the first generation of Jewish kids in the U.S. who answered their Yiddish-speaking parents in English only.)

But even the families whose children agree to speak English have a thorny path to tread. One of the most common of all problems is that the child of English-speaking parents never quite fits into his proper English class. He may not yet know how to read or write, but he's still light-years ahead of his classmates who are learning things like, "I am a pupil. This is a table. She is a 'gorl'."

If a school has enough English-speaking children of approximately the same age, they may form special classes for *"dovrei anglit"* — English speakers. But this is the exception, not the rule. If, however, a child is taught to read and write at home, what is he supposed to do when everyone else is sitting in that English class? Wander around the schoolyard? Neither principals nor teachers nor parents like that idea, although the kids don't seem to mind. On the other hand, keeping an English speaker (even a borderline one) in class makes for constant discipline problems. There are undoubtedly ways of dealing with this, but no one seems to have discovered them yet.

The ironic result is that the English-speaking child who has a definite head start often ends up way behind. The other kids may start from scratch, but they progress in a normal, orderly fashion and, eventually, they arrive somewhere, while the kid who was somewhere in the first place, left the class and got lost along the way. Our very own Son Number Four, for example.

When he was ten, I discovered (completely by accident) that his class had already learned how to read and write the alphabet. (At that time, children in Israeli schools started learning English as a second language in fifth grade.) But not my son. "Why not?" I asked rather threateningly. "Because," he answered confidently, "I already know English good so I don't need that class!"

Many Americans insist on speaking only English in their homes. Even if the children persist in answering in Hebrew, you can assume that at the very least, they will understand. In our home, we didn't follow this particular plan of action. We felt comfortable with the constant drift into Hebrew, and sticking to English on principle seemed forced and unnatural, perhaps because we're sort of partial to the Hebrew language. After all, it is *Hashem's* own *"mama loshen"* and we use it all the time, from *Modeh Ani* in the morning until *Krias Shema* at night.

Hebrew, you see, has such a nice feel to it. It sounds so . . . well, so Jewish, and it seems like such a wonderful way to speak to Jewish kids. If it was good enough for Avraham, Yitzchak, Yaakov, Moshe, David, Shlomo and a few more, I figure it's good enough for us, too.

However, I did want the kids to know some English, so I often found myself a bit schizophrenic . . . sometimes speaking one language and sometimes the other . . . and sometimes a mixture of both. The resulting jumble ("Hebrish" is what we called it) was not bilingual, but semi-lingual at best.

For example, in our house, when I would say to someone, "Are you going out? Can you take the garbage?" I'd get an answer like this: "I not going out now. I going later. I can't to help you. Can't X (here you insert the name of a brother or sister) take it now?"

Note: There is no Hebrew equivalent of the verb "to be" in the present tense, so the kids omitted it when speaking English. Yet, they did put in the infinitive (as in "to help") where it didn't belong, because that's the way it's used in Hebrew.

When confronted with clear-cut evidence of some domestic crime, our boys would say something like "I didn't did it!"

while our young daughter, charming and full of innocence, would add, "I didn't did it either. Anybody did it!" ("Anybody" was always getting into mischief in our house. I used to threaten that if I ever caught up with him, I'd be brutal, but I never did uncover his identity.)

In the hope that she would have a better command of English than her brothers seemed to possess, my husband and I tried speaking only English to our daughter. The result of that experiment was havoc. The boys all assumed that she did not understand Hebrew and they insisted on conversing with her in their ear-shattering English, even when her Hebrew was perfect.

She, as a sign of appreciation for their efforts, adopted their marvelous brand of English. "Mommy say you not to do it. The boys is being not good now. Mommy, where is you? To where you going? How I can open the door by myself?" Ad infinitum.

Our eldest son was four when we came on *aliyah*. Perhaps that helped to explain the fact that he alone spoke English fairly well and fluently, albeit with an accent. But he had a strong aversion to reading in English, even though he read Hebrew voraciously. Try as we might, we could not convince him that it was important or worthwhile to slave away for hours, laboriously reading a book in English, when he could finish it off effortlessly and in one tenth the time in the Hebrew translation.

Another problem which caused us untold suffering was the communication gap. I'd give a child simple instructions about something in English and then, just to be on the safe side, I'd ask, "Do you understand?" Answer: "Yes. Now tell me in *Ivrit.* I hear you better in *Ivrit.*"

Aside from grammar and communication problems, there were other difficulties which we constantly encountered. Like the things my kids expected me to know in Hebrew, but which I didn't. A prime example was New Math. (In those days they thought they had discovered something new about teaching old arithmetic. They've since discovered that no one, including the teachers, understood what they were doing, and schools are now returning to the old tried and true methods.)

Now I do not claim to be a mathematician, but I did make A's in high school algebra and geometry and I passed a basic college math course. But working out 7th grade New Math in Hebrew really taxed my powers. Subjects like math and music are supposed to be international and know no language barriers, but it's not true. I'd explain away in English and Son Number One would say he didn't understand. So I'd switch to Hebrew. Then he'd say it didn't make sense.

But lest you think my children were self-conscious about their imperfect English, let me assure you that you are mistaken. They all grew up secure in the knowledge that they were beautifully bilingual. So much so, that one day, Son Number Four (who knew English "so good") came home very proud of himself. He had assisted a tourist in finding an address and the man told him he sounded "just like an American!" My husband's comment was that the man's hearing aid was obviously not in good working order.

Intriguingly, from somewhere within their foreign-sounding Hebrish, you could still detect a long, drawn-out midwestern accent, an inheritance from my husband and myself. Once, a stranger speaking to the boys correctly surmised that either they or their parents had come from the Midwest. As far as they were concerned, if this wasn't proof of how marvelous their English was, then what did constitute proof? At that point, I gave up.

After all, how many Israeli families can say "Thirty purple birds, sitting on a curb, burping and chirping and eating dirty worms," even if it is with an accent?

We also used to work on "Thirty-three thrushes, thrashing through the thistles," but I must admit, we never got further than "Ferty free froshes." Some things are just "roff goink" from beginning to end.

There was, however, one major compensation for our kids' faulty English: their Hebrew. How long and hard our generation had worked at translating *Chumash* and *Navi* and *Tefillah* into English so that we could understand the words. Our kids picked up a *siddur* and knew from the first what they were saying. They went through the *Chumash* in the original, instead of from a translation (or even worse, a Bible comic book!) They played word games and told stories based on Jewish sources, instead of on the Brothers Grimm (*lehavdil*). During their games of marbles or hide and seek, they rattled off phrases used by the *tanaim* and *amoraim*, and sang hundreds of songs from the repertoire of David Hamelech. (They understood the words, too!) After twenty-five years in Israel (and despite my better-than-average Hebrew), I am still jealous of the linguistic ease with which they move through the *mekoros* — the *Tanach*, the *mefarshim*, the *tefillos.* G-d's language is their own, which is as it should be.

❀ ❀ ❀

There is an intrinsic *kedushah* in Hebrew which other languages do not have; a certain purity which makes it a more fitting language for a Jew to think and speak in, and certainly more fitting for praying to G-d. Hebrew lends itself more easily to higher realms of thought and feeling. And since language shapes our thoughts and feelings by giving them form, it does make a difference which language (and what kind of language!) we use.

❀ ❀ ❀

It still makes me wince when I remember "I didn't did it!" and I'm sure that some parents have had more success in raising grammatical English offspring. But the truth of the matter is, I'm happy and grateful to have raised a family which speaks to G-d — and to man — in *Lashon Hakodesh.*

# Kids: A Public Commodity

srael is a land of babies and it's quite obvious why. The Torah tells us in a perfectly plain and forth-right fashion that if, in the Land of Israel, we walk in G-d's ways, carefully keeping His statutes, laws, and commandments, He will turn His face towards us, make us fruitful, multiply us, and establish His covenant with us. Even though we haven't quite learned how to "walk" properly in His ways as yet, fortunately for us, *Hashem* is patient and merciful and very generous about advancing us credit.

So throughout the country, wherever you go, you see a world of children. Women with children and women about to have children. Women pushing buggies and strollers, and stores which sell them — together with cribs and dressers and bassinets and potties. Children's clothes, toys and shoes are big business, even when business is slow. And the busiest municipal departments are always the pre-kindergarten/

kindergarten divisions. There are no two ways about it. Israel is a child-oriented society. *Baruch Hashem.*

It does, however, take some getting used to, because your baby isn't only yours in the Holy Land. Once you've had it, it becomes communal property, a fact you will discover as soon as you walk out the front door. Did the little darling squeak? Someone will comment. Did he cry? Someone will investigate. Is it hot out? Or cold? Don't worry. Someone will instruct you and tell you what to do.

"Give him a drink." "Put his hat on;." "Take his hat off." "He's tired, hungry, thirsty, teething." "Give him water." "Give him juice." "Take his sweater off; he's hot." "Put the sweater on; it's cold." "Doesn't he have a hat? It's windy and his ears will hurt."

They'll ask who your doctor is, how much the baby weighs, if he sleeps through the night. And you're expected to answer.

Even an outing with a smiling baby is a public affair. On a quick, fifteen-minute walk to the neighborhood drugstore with her six-month-old daughter, one young woman I know was stopped a total of nine times. Four times by neighbors; three times by elderly people she did not know; and twice by kids. All stopped her to comment on how adorable the baby was. Admittedly, hers is cute, but nine times in fifteen minutes shows an enormous amount of public interest in the younger generation!

Once, on a bus ride in Jerusalem, a screaming baby refused to be comforted. The resulting chaos had to be seen to be believed. Old men and women from all parts of the bus gave advice and directions; people passed food and drinks to the mother; the bus driver wanted to turn the radio up ("Maybe some music will soothe him?"); teenagers were willing to walk the infant up and down the aisle. So what did you expect from a busload of Jewish grandparents and parents and kids? Cool and detached we aren't.

I personally know of four separate emergency cases where

people were flagged down and ended up taking expectant mothers to the hospital — women they had never seen before — and having deposited their uninvited passengers at the door of the delivery room, each one parked his car, went into the hospital and waited patiently to find out if he had "delivered" a boy or a girl. If it was a boy, he came to the *bris,* too.

The Israeli government participates in births. *Bituach Leumi* (the Israeli version of Social Security) gives a gift of several hundred shekel to each new baby, plus a monthly sum for each child until the age of sixteen. The Jerusalem municipality sends a colorful certificate for a J.N.F. tree planted in honor of each baby. Many stores, organizations, community centers, and schools take the number of children in a family into consideration when billing a client.

In our neighborhood, elderly men going to or from *shul* in the morning are regularly accompanied by neighborhood kids on their way to school. Conversation ensues; smiles are exchanged; and a bit of candy or gum is passed into eager hands. A little love and communication between the generations is a nice way to start the day, both for the elderly and for the young.

The most heart-warming display of children, however, is during *chol hamoed* when Israeli families turn out en masse. The majority are either hiking or driving or picnicking or visiting with their kids. In the religious neighborhoods you can see long strings of hand-holding brothers and sisters helping each other to cross the streets or to see the animals in the zoo or to kiss the *Kotel* or to buy an ice cream cone.

Just as the Prophet Zecharya promised, our children — the offspring of Avraham Avinu — are filling the streets of *Eretz Yisrael.* "And the streets of the City shall be filled with little boys and girls playing . . . and if it be a marvel in the eyes of the remnants of the people in those days, it shall also be a marvel in My eyes, says *Hashem Tzevakos.*"

It is a marvel indeed. *Ken yirbu.*

# Sons and Soldiers
# In the Holy Land

t's not exactly what we had in mind when we heard those beautiful words at his *bris* . . . *l'gadlo l'Torah, l'chupah, ul'maasim tovim* — may you be privileged to raise him to greatness in Torah, to the marriage canopy, and to good deeds. Nor is it exactly what I dreamt of all the years he was growing up. But life has its own ornery way of arranging things, and one day, shortly before his engagement, our twenty-one-year-old son enlisted in a special army program for *bachurai yeshivah*. (After three months of basic training and three months of active duty, these young men are required to remain in the yeshivah or in one of several other authorized areas — such as education —

for an additional eight years. They also do their regular, annual reserve duty.)

Our son joined a combat unit, and normal mother that I am, I was not completely cool, calm or collected at the prospect. But I found myself upset for a different, unexpected reason.

It didn't begin at the beginning. We sent our son off with kisses, smiles, a few silent tears and prayers and lots of cheerful advice. It began a few days later, when he returned home for the first time in uniform. Properly outfitted as a member in good standing of Tzahal, the Israeli army, he was donning a spanking new uniform with appropriate insignias and was toting a heavy duffel bag stuffed with khaki clothing. Slung over his shoulder was one long, heavy rifle.

To understand my sudden chagrin, I must explain that I have never been enthusiastic about metal objects, especially military metal. For me, airplanes, tanks, even trains and cars — and surely guns! — are not objects of admiration. In fact, when our boys were young, we were the kind of parents who objected to toy guns on principle (except for Purim, when we gave in to his dreams of becoming a cowboy). Living in Israel for so many years, the sight of guns on soldiers, border police and settlers was not strange. But to the best of my memory, no gun had ever been inside our peaceful home. Which was just fine with me.

Suddenly, here was my gentle, quiet, kind, considerate, sensitive son, the one who literally wouldn't hurt a fly, with a long, dark, ugly piece of metal designed to kill. And just to drive home the fact that this was not a Purim accessory, it came with a clip of live ammunition.

Here was a child we had raised to be a *talmid chacham,* a *ben Torah,* a doer of good deeds; perhaps a teacher or a doctor. His tools would be books, not guns. His ammunition would be Torah, wisdom, and love, not bullets. His job was to bring life to the world and not, G-d forbid, to kill. As his sister and brothers excitedly ran for their cameras to photograph their newly-soldiered brother, I went to my room and cried.

As basic training progressed, I continued to feel like a creature apart. Other mothers worried about the rough conditions, the lack of sleep, the relentless discipline and the exhausting physical exertion which pushed the kids to the limit of their tolerance (and then some). In short, they were walking around like zombies.

I took a more pragmatic view. Tzahal couldn't be too hard on them or they wouldn't continue to function. Knowing that the army had a vested interest in keeping my son at least nominally alive and healthy during the months of basic training, I decided to refrain from maternal hysteria. I kept him supplied with edibles from the house, clean underwear, and perhaps I tended to stay home more than usual, waiting, I suppose, for a surprise telephone call or visit.

But my real concern was future-oriented. What would my son be doing after his basic training? The answer came all too soon. He was sent into Lebanon. When it was noisy, messy, and very unpleasant.

My reaction to combat duty was to become the proverbial ostrich. I didn't listen to the news. I didn't read the paper. Every time people (especially mothers) met and discussed what we refer to here as "the *matzav*" — the situation — I pretended that all this talk about fighting had nothing to do with me. My son was fine. I had no idea where he was or what he was doing, so he obviously couldn't be doing anything very important (I mean, if he were, I would know, wouldn't I?). No news is good news, and every day with no news was a day to be blessed.

Of course my not listening to the news was in itself a sign that not all was normal and well, for the average Israeli listens to the news at least four or five times a day.

It wasn't that I was worried about my son's physical welfare. I did worry about that, too, of course, hard and long. I prayed and hoped that *Hakadosh Baruch Hu* would protect and take care of him and every one of his friends and that they all would remain safe and sound. Further than that I did not dare to plan or think.

But in addition to the "normal" worries (which were worries enough), something else was troubling me. I kept wondering what these kids were doing. I knew that war-related activities were not exactly fun and games, but I simply could not envision my son actually shooting that cannon he was responsible for. Or that submachine gun he now *shlepped* around with him (he had graduated from the rifle). Perhaps I could see him shooting it, but surely not at people!

I know this may sound ridiculous. What is war about, if not killing when necessary? Nonetheless, it was one thing to think about war in the abstract, and something very different to have your own offspring involved in it!

One *Shabbos* when he was home, he spoke about what he and his friends were "doing." I listened to every word, but nothing seemed to fit. It sounded like some strange scenario where someone had mixed up all the players. Imagining these fine, young, lovely (and they really are lovely, every one of the kids I had met) boys-turned-men in the midst of killing and death, was like watching some crazy disco dance full of flashing lights and crashing noises. It was a world gone mad. What was my son doing there?

I asked him if he was as discomfited as I. He thought for a moment, and then, quiet but determined, he answered "No." He explained that neither he nor the army at large had any interest in killing, which was, after all, not their purpose. They were an Army of Defense, engaged in protecting people. Their own people, their own land.

The world we live in is often brutal and ruthless, and *sin'as Esav,* that eternal and instinctive hatred of Jacob's seed, is still going strong. In each generation its targets and methods are different, but its goals remain the same: weakening, damaging or destroying *Am Yisrael* — its physical body, its spiritual condition. Even lowering our morale, our sense of purpose or joy, is, for our enemies, an objective worth pursuing.

In our own times, one of the goals of *sin'as Esav* is the destruction, G-d forbid, of the Jewish presence in the Jewish Land. Infused with a passionate hatred, they are determined to destroy what we have built and to prevent our building further. The fulfillment of Divine promises to the Jewish people does not sit well with the forces of evil in the world.

Therefore, he continued, in the "them or us" situations he found himself in, there was not even a second's hesitation in his mind that "us" took precedence. And he reminded me . . . *mi shemiracheim al achzarim, sofo l'hisachzor al rachmanim.* He who has pity on ruthless people will eventually be ruthless to people of compassion.

※　※　※

There was no hatred, no extremism in his voice. He spoke without any *shvitz* or swagger, but with quiet determination and much *emunah.* At that point, I stopped worrying about what he and his friends were "doing." The Jew and the soldier were one, and the Jew was definitely in control.

※　※　※

There is another side to the story too. Being the parent of a soldier is an unusual experience which opens up new vistas and greatly expands one's social consciousness. I suddenly discovered that I had many "sons." All those kids going back to their bases on Sunday mornings, waiting for a hitch on the roads, somehow became "mine." It wasn't theoretical either. I had always noticed them, of course, but now I felt differently about them. I knew their mothers were home worrying about them, just as I was worrying about my son. I knew what their bases looked liked, what inconveniences they had to put up with, what dangers many of them had to face. I knew that even the ones with easy jobs on base were putting off their plans for life for three long years because *Am Yisrael* needs them. And I knew that the combat kids were putting their lives on the line to help keep Jews alive and well, just as my son was doing.

I became more involved with them. I noticed a kid in uniform more quickly. I cared about them. When it was cold or raining, I thought of them immediately, wondering if their pup tents were dripping or holding up in the wind. In the summer *chamsin,* instead of complaining how hot I was, I wondered if the kids were remembering to drink enough. Observant or not, Ashkenazi, Sefardi — it didn't make any difference what they were. If they were Jewish kids in uniform, they were mine.

This feeling of *kol Yisrael areivim zeh bazeh* — of mutual responsibility — forms a great part of the social glue in Israel. It is an unspoken tie which binds a highly heterogeneous population, living in close proximity, in a very small country. No one is more individualistic than the Jew. (Just think of the classic Jewish joke about two Jews on an island with their three synagogues.) But in this one area, we're all in the same boat; our kids are standing shoulder to shoulder, together, doing their part to protect us all. Your kid helps guarantee my kid's safety and vice versa. We are, indeed, brothers.

Even families who do not have a son in the army will have someone they know or care about who is serving. A nephew or cousin or neighbor, or your son-in-law's brother. But everyone cares about the kids they don't know as well (and if they don't, they should,) for they are all the children of Avraham Avinu. When things go along relatively quietly and normally, this feeling of mutual responsibility and care is taken for granted. But in times of crisis or stress, it comes immediately to the fore.

❦ ❦ ❦

Like all good Jewish mothers, I am proud of my Sons —
my own private sons and my communal sons as well.
Although they may not be perfect (who is?), they are special
nonetheless. And their willingness to give years of their
young lives to protecting *Am Yisrael* will undoubtedly earn
them many points in G-d's Heavenly Accountings. The fact
that so many of them do this so often, for so long, and with so
little complaint — whatever their background or understanding of Jewish values — is a wonder indeed.

❦ ❦ ❦

May the day come soon when Jewish mothers and fathers
need not worry about soldier-sons; when their rifles and
machine guns and cannons are turned into plowshares; and
when all Jewish parents are privileged to lead their sons, not
to an army, but only "to *Torah,* to *chuppah* and to *maasim
tovim.*"

# The Pluses of Buses and What Else is New?

ho's doing what in your town, what's going on when and where, and how do you find out? Perhaps you read the paper or listen to the news. But for the average Israeli, news, like everything else, takes a more personal, direct route. In true Biblical fashion, as we "sit in our homes or walk along our ways; when we lie down to rest and when we arise," we are confronted with our news. Nor do I mean the political or economic or world news; I mean *our* news. The vital information we need about sales, strikes, services, doctors, repairs, cessation of vital utilities like water, phone service, gas and electricity. In short, whatever we need to know about, for and from our neighborhood (and neighbors) in order to function.

The most immediate, efficient and informative source of information is children, and the younger the better. I don't know how they do it, but they are always the first to know about babies, pregnancies, engagements, weddings, and people moving in and out of the neighborhood. And, of course they know exactly which school everyone is in, which grade, and who their teacher is. They'll tell you what everyone's father does, where the family went for vacation last year, how many of the kids are married, to whom, and where they live. They bring their information right into the house, too, so you don't even have to leave your kitchen.

Other harborers of information are the taxis and trucks with loudspeakers attached to them. Usually, they are selling watermelons and ice cream, but they also announce funerals, fire-sales, and demonstrations (of which we have many). Once in a while, we even still get the *"alte zachen"* men (buyers of second-hand merchandise) — nowadays, they are usually Arabs — coming through with their plaintive *"Aaalte Zaaach'n"* cry.

If you can get yourself out of the house and down to your mailbox, you'll find it stuffed with flyers and brochures announcing sales, repair jobs, services and stores; needy people and institutions, and kids looking for jobs. You'll also probably find a few announcements stuck to the walls in the hall.

Your walk to the bus stop is creatively decorated as well. Trees and billboards and the bus-stop itself all sport . . . you guessed it . . . more of the same. Plus ads for apartments for sale and rent and many Lost and Found notices.

But beyond this point, the emphasis changes. Having covered most of the written news, you are now about to enter the Land of Speech. Younger mothers sit in the park, and while their offspring are busy on the swings and slides, they are on the benches catching up and swapping items of interest with other mothers of similar disposition.

Then there is the *makolet* group which meets in the grocery and gathers tidbits along with food. But the men have it best of all. They meet, not once, but three times a day for their daily portion of What's New. On the way to *shul,* of course. You can see them talking, as they go back and forth in two's or three's or four's in the morning and late afternoon. I like to think of the casual strollers as having a more philosophic bent, the argumentative types as the military planners and advisers, the jokers as the politicians, and the latecomers hurrying along as being either the really busy people — or the less organized ones! Chances are, anyone who isn't talking on the way to *shul,* is talking on the way back.

❀ ❀ ❀

But there is no doubt that the buses are the champions in promoting interpersonal communication among the populace. In a hodge-podge of languages too. (I once counted seven different languages being spoken on the bus I was riding, plus one I didn't recognize at all.) And unlike big cities in the U.S., you do speak to your fellow passengers. (Just try to make an innocuous comment to a someone on a New York subway and see how fast they move away!)

There seems to be so much to say on our buses, too. They are clearing-houses for opinions. We comment on the weather, the news, fellow passengers. We instruct and educate and empathize.

"Isn't anyone going to help that lady with the baby?"

"Little boy, get up and give that old man a seat! Didn't you learn about honoring the elderly? What do they teach you in school nowadays?"

"Don't wake up that poor soldier. So what if he's taking up two seats? Can't you see how tired he is? Poor kid, he's probably going through basic training. Let him sleep!"

The drivers are part of the lively give-and-take as well. While some of them tend to be dictatorial, running "their" bus as they see fit, if they anger their passengers, things get vocal.

"You're driving like a madman! Slow down!"

"Why didn't you stop at that station and pick up those kids? There's room for them in the bus!"

"Change the radio station, will you?"

"No, don't!"

"Turn the news up, please."

"It's too loud. Turn it down."

"Turn it off! Who wants to hear it?"

I've received recipes and crocheting instructions from utter strangers on the bus; have been instructed on how to raise my children (and have given a few instructions in return); have been sold two sets of brand-new sheets; was invited to a wedding; and almost made a *shidduch* (it wasn't the bus's fault that it didn't work out).

I found that riding on buses and trains in America was nerve-wracking. They are so quiet. All they do is take you where you want to go.

❅  ❅  ❅

Each Jerusalem bus line has its own flavor and style, and each provides a different show. Our bus passes the Machaneh Yehudah *shuk* — the big outdoor market — and quickly fills up with people *shlepping* fruits, vegetables, and freshly slaughtered chickens. We also boast a fine selection of the latest American fashions modeled by the American girls studying at schools in our neighborhood.

Some bus lines carry a disproportionate number of blind people, or deaf children, or *kollel* men, or Arabs, or religious Jews, or people going to Hadassah hospital. The lines going to and from the Central Bus Station on Friday afternoons and Sunday mornings are full of soldiers who head home for *Shabbat* leave. The exact scene depends on the route, and it makes for colorful traveling.

Despite the proliferation of cars in Israel, people still use buses to transport all sorts of bulky and unwieldy items. I've seen people board the buses with canaries in cages, fish in plastic bags full of water, television sets, feather pillows, bicycles, sets of dishes, *sukkah* slats, and whatever else they think the driver will let them get away with.

The back of the bus belongs, of course to the Buggy Brigade. There is even a special seat-less area for buggies and strollers opposite the rear doors. (Do women with buggies ever travel on American buses?)

In short, to plug into the real communications center in Israel, Egged is the name of the game. It's not advertised in the tourist brochures, but once inside, a bus-ride provides an Israeli experience deluxe. And at bargain prices too!

# A Long-lasting Love

 don't know about anyone else, but from the moment I first set foot in *Eretz Yisrael*, I was a lost cause. I still remember very vividly how excited, how awed, how humbled and how punch-drunk I felt. Every step of the way, from the plane until we unpacked in Jerusalem, I had to keep pinching myself to make sure it was true. I had finally arrived.

That was over thirty years ago, but the feeling is still with me. Every time I look around, each time I travel within the country, whenever I visit someplace different or new — I am filled with gratitude and amazement that I am here. (And, may I add, whenever I am elsewhere, in *chutz la'Aretz*, no matter how lovely a time I am having, and no matter how wonderful people are, I always experience a nagging feeling of not being "home.")

Jerusalem, of course, has it all. On a walk through Shaarei Chessed, one of the older sections of the city, I noticed a ceramic plaque at the entrance of a newly renovated house. It quoted the verse from tractate *Nedarim*: *There are three groups of people who will merit the World to Come.* He who lives in *Eretz Yisrael* was the first. It was a nice finishing touch for a new home in an old land.

A trip to the northern Galil, for example, or the southern Negev, leaves me elated with the scenery, the smells, the history, the *Jewishness* of it all. Whenever we travel, I watch the neat, rich fields fly past the window of the car and I try to imagine what it all looked like sixty, eighty, one hundred years ago. When waves of pioneers came, and through superhuman effort and great *emunah* (even if the pioneers did not always define it in these terms), they did the seemingly impossible, restoring a desolate, deserted, barren land into a land of plenty — the ancient Promised Land flowing with milk and honey.

Each summer we spend a few days at a cousin's moshav in the far north. Today, it is a beautiful, lush, luxurious place. But on our cousin's desk is a picture of the site when he came to it a mere forty years ago. Rocky land, not a building in sight; wild, scraggly growth; and . . . tents. I look at the picture each summer; then I look out the window. The contrast is hard to digest.

Israel's early pioneers could only have accomplished what they did with the help of Divine blessings, yet there is no denying their part in the miracle, and I am left awed, and grateful.

And of course walking through the Land of the Bible is no experience to be sneezed at. One might think that spiritual proximity with G-d and His Torah is sufficient, without any physical trappings, but if *Hakadosh Baruch Hu* Himself commanded us to live in a very specific physical setting in order to best carry out His will (which is what the *mitzvah* of living in *Eretz Yisrael* is all about), then who am I to argue?

This feeling of being at one with the country is more than a state of mind. Like the country itself, it is almost a physical phenomenon. Think of the universal Israeli desire to hike and tour. *Eretz Yisrael* is a place one has to see, to touch, to walk over and through, to personally know. And why shouldn't it be so, if *Chazal* said that "he who walks four cubits in *Eretz Yisrael* merits the World to Come"? Obviously, there's a lot of World to Come connected with this particular part of the universe!

Nowadays, in our instant world, tourists come and go, confident that they have "seen" and "done" the country in ten days or two weeks. A spin through the city, a snap of the camera, and off you go to the next place on the map. Maybe I'm slow, but after twenty-five years, I'm still discovering new places and people and rediscovering old ones. And savoring them all.

❀   ❀   ❀

We have a private family fantasy concerning our national real estate. Not being able to financially afford much of it, we have nonetheless appropriated large sections for our personal use. My sister "owns" a large, rolling tract of land near Emek Ayalon, the valley where Joshua stilled the sun and the moon in their heavenly tracks. She has declared it her own summer-dream estate. I "acquired" a lovely plot of land outside the city of Tzefat, high in the mountains. Someone else decided to adopt as his own a cliff, overlooking the deep valley from Metulla (the northernmost point in the country) down to Kiryat Shemona. We agreed to keep Lake Kinneret communal property since there was no possibility of dividing its particular beauty in a fair manner.

I also received a special dispensation to expropriate a small piece of Jerusalem for my personal dreams. In the inner city, on a quiet, leafy street with low, red-roofed houses. While I did not obtain permission from any of the owners on the street, I doubt if my mentally "moving in" caused any commotion. The rest of Yerushalayim, of course, we left as a National Heritage Site.

Two of our children decided that they wanted more daily contact with their dream-estate fantasies. One of them chose to live with his family near the ancient Jewish city of Azza, in a southern moshav right next to the sea. An area of clear blue skies, deep blue water, and clean, golden sand, it is surrounded with graceful palm trees and is full of the sounds of Jewish children in school and at play. Another offspring moved outside Jerusalem where he and his wife can see a stunning, wild, desert landscape from one window, the rooftops of Jerusalem from another, and the local yeshivah and *shul* from their porch.

The point of all this is that the Land of Israel is terribly personal. Once, while spending a few days in Switzerland, I marveled at the beauty of the country. It was like seeing a magnificent child — someone else's. But when you turn to your own child — the child whom you see through the eyes of your love — the picture is completely different. The other kid is undoubtedly gorgeous, but yours is ... well, not just beautiful, but miraculously precious and unique.

Which is why you can't really compare the Judean Hills to the Alps. G-d created all mountains and made them beautiful, but He descended upon and blessed the Judean Mountains with His Spirit.

You might say we have our own special spectacles for seeing here. Dirt, for example, is dirt. Everywhere. But in Israel? Ah ... now that's *holy* dirt! Water is water, and wet to boot. But water in Israel? That's a blessing! Sand is sand and rocks are rocks. But in the Negev or the Judean desert? There they become Jewish history. And a mountain is an elevation which usually looks glorious. But the Judean or Galilean Mountains, or the Golan Heights? Why, they are the personal footstools of the Almighty Himself!

And so I look out my window daily at the busy, bustling city of Jerusalem and I breathe a quiet, private prayer. A prayer of thanksgiving for the good fortune of being here; and a prayer of requests for the future. For the future well-being of G-d's city and His Land; for His Temple, as yet unbuilt; for His people living in the Land. And for the welfare of the rest of His children who are not yet here.

# SoulScan

## A Jewish Point of View

> . . . for the ways of God are straight.
> The righteous walk in them,
> while the rebellious stumble in them.
> *Hoshea 14:10.*

*Learning to walk — and talk and think and act — without stumbling is no mean feat. You'd think that if it only takes a dozen or so months for a baby to learn to walk, an intelligent teen or a mature adult would get the rest of the process under control in a similarly short period. But no; once we've learned how to use our feet, we spend the rest of our lives learning how to use our brains and our hearts and our tongues, and sometimes, even a lifetime isn't enough to master the art.*

*So we stumble along, and despite our frequent falls, we rise and go on. And somehow, step by step, through a combination of trial and tribulation laced with joy, we learn to walk.*

*But walking isn't sufficient. We must learn to climb as well, each one up his own personal ladder, its feet planted firmly on the ground; its head reaching to the heavens. Our effort is rewarded, for as soon as we begin our ascent, the view changes; it gets clearer and brighter and more invigorating. More Jewish, you might say.*

*There are many ways to walk and to climb, to speak and think and act — as many as there are people in the world. May your particular walk be quick, your steps sure, and once you've climbed a bit, don't forget to enjoy the view!*

# A Smile Makes the World Go Round

hy is it that seeing some people for the first time elicits an immediate, positive, warm reaction, while seeing others, for no apparent reason, leaves you feeling perfectly chilly? What is there in the human physiognomy which can produce such an instinctive warming (or cooling) in the heart of the beholder? The answer may well be smile lines.

When you've spent your life smiling at the world because you find it a pleasant, goodly place, your attitude becomes imprinted on your face. And which of us is immune to a friendly soul, a kindly heart, a happy, positive personality? Lines on the face have been described as "character marks," and they are indeed.

I often wonder if the *gedolim* cards so arduously collected by schoolboys are really a positive educational experience. Most of the pictures look so solemn and glum. (Ditto for a good many of the illustrations of famous rabbis in books.) I don't believe for one minute that this is the aura these holy men exuded! With contemporary *rabbanim* there is at least a chance of finding a more sympathetic pose. But pity the poor rabbis who lived before the era of instant photography. They are forever engraved in our minds as brooding, unsmiling, melancholy men of the spirit.

One smiling rabbinical luminary lives on our block. He is a joy to behold. On his daily walks to and from shul, he greets everyone he meets — men, women and children — with a warm, wide smile and a cheerful "*Shalom.*" Not only are you convinced that he thinks highly of you and is absolutely delighted to see you, you instinctively want to be the kind of person you hope he thinks you are! I always think of him as a living example of *hevey mekabel kol adam b'sever panim yafos* — Greet every person with a pleasant face.

A smile has power not only to make you feel good, but to actually help you act better. I remember a bus driver by the name of Seri who drove the line in our neighborhood. His was always a bus full of happy people. Upon entering, each passenger was greeted with a smile, a joke, or a friendly word, and their faces beamed with simple pleasure as they filed into the back of the bus. They smiled at each other too, full of happy comments on the day, the weather, the state of affairs. Never was a sharp word or an argument heard on Seri's bus. People were even known to wait for his run, even if it meant letting another bus or two pass them by. He retired several years ago, but people still speak about him as though he were a close friend. He helped us start each day *b'darchey noam* — with pleasant ways — *ub'sever panim yafos*, and we were grateful.

In an effort to educate their students *b'darchey noam*, a

school in Jerusalem held a Smiling Campaign one year in the month of *Adar* — the month of joy. The children were asked to smile at people they passed in the streets (the streets of Jerusalem being somewhat safer than the streets of New York) and then to report on the reactions. It was a rather amazing project. The kids were overwhelmed with good wishes, kind words, smiles and helpful adults. Several fine friendships materialized as a result.

Just think of how we melt at the smile of a baby or a young child. And how much more — and more easily — we learn from a smiling teacher. Why stretching one's mouth in a slightly upward position should lead straight to the heart of humankind is a mystery.

Instead of smiling, we could have been programmed to shrug our shoulders or twiddle our thumbs as a sign of love and affection. Yet it is the mouth which performs several vital, amazing functions: bringing the outside world into our bodies in the form of food; bringing our innermost thoughts and feelings to the outside world in the form of speech; and expressing love — that miraculous bonding of our innermost selves and the world outside — in the form of a word, a kiss, a smile.

A friend described an argument she once had with a particularly irascible acquaintance. For months, the women remained angry. My friend did not want the argument to continue any longer, but since she considered herself the wronged party, she couldn't quite bring herself to do the apologizing either. So she worked out a simple strategy . Every time she saw the other woman or passed her in the street, she would smile and say hello. Within weeks, the ice broke. A few words were exchanged here and there; a *kiddush* invitation was extended at the birth of a baby; and eventually a proper peace was made. The other woman admitted to her that if she had not been smiled at so frequently, she would have remained a sworn non-friend for life.

Smiles are worth money. They earn millions. Imagine all of the media ads, but without the smiling faces. The attraction-quota all but disappears.

Someone should open a *Gemach* — a free loan fund — for smiles. If it's praiseworthy to lend money, dishes, and various other items as a *mitzvah*-related activity, how much more so to provide a little free joy to those who need it. There's no question that we could all use a few additional smiles per day. And what a cost-efficient product to dispense! It takes no capital to provide and needs no storage space; there's no breakage or depreciation, nothing to spoil or go out of style. It's always fresh and is easily available in assorted sizes, according to need.

If, as they say, the eyes are the windows to the soul, then a smile is undoubtedly the highway to the heart. Happy traveling!

# G-d Bless All the Jews

hen I was a little girl, I used to think the world was divided into two kinds of people — Jews and gentiles.

Then I learned that there were different kinds of Jews. Some Jews were Rumanian (the kind on my mother's side). They weren't quite the cream, but definitely tolerable. (This from my father's side.) The better quality, more elite Jews, were Lithuanians — Litvakim. (This also from my father's side). Chassidim, so they told me way back then, were a third kind, but I bumped into them only on occasion and by accident, and they were obviously (so I heard from impeccable sources) from another track completely.

As I grew up, I realized that this was a rather simplistic view of the situation. Nevertheless, our sheltered midwestern existence brought us into contact with very few other types of

Jews, except perhaps for an occasional exotic Yemenite who wandered mistakenly out our way. It was only upon my engagement to what, at the time, I thought was an ordinary American Jew, that I discovered the Hungarians, who came, so it seemed, mixed in with a lot of chassidim. Like under my *chupah.*

Most brides have tender memories (if they remember anything at all) of their wedding celebrations. I remember laughing. Under the *chupah* yet. But seeing my Litvishe father, *z"l*, standing next to Chicago's three chassidishe rebbes (complete with *shtreimlach* in honor of the occasion), all of whom were helping officiate, was . . . well, it was the kind of thing that brings a warm, wide smile to a Jewish face, at least to mine. (My father-in-law, *z"l*, was the president of one of the aforementioned rebbe's *shteiblach*). The funniest part of all was that I don't think my father even minded.

Since then, I've discovered that I feel quite at home among the *shtreimel* crowd (if I may be so flippant — no slight intended, as you will see if you keep reading). I've also become good friends with several ladies from chassidishe dynasties of repute, and when one of them told me several years ago that the entire Jewish people would eventually take on a definite chassidishe hue, I smiled condescendingly (although I couldn't help wondering if perhaps she knew something I didn't. . .).

Not all chassidim are Hungarians, of course; nor are all Hungarians chassidim, although the two do seem to go hand in hand. But even the Hungarians who aren't chassidim are a vivacious bunch. They have a certain *joie de vivre* — if you can only understand what they're saying.

In Hebrew, many Hungarians have successfully obliterated both the past and future tenses from the language, together with the masculine, feminine and plural genders. They speak in a monotensal, monosexual present, modified with adjectives and pronouns, just enough to make a little sense of things. It's a neat, painless (to the speaker, if not to the listener) form of pidgin (as in "I go today. You go yesterday. They go tomorrow.") I have dozens of lovely Hungarian cousins in Israel (my husband's contribution to our family) and my only regret is that I find it so hard to understand what some of them are saying.

Hungarians do things in a big way, whether it's eating or dressing or killing a language. Or being religious (usually very) or non-religious (usually very). Or being warm and kind, which I have found them to be very much of. There's nothing halfway about Hungary.

But to get back to the chassidim . . . blood runs deep. My thoroughly Americanized husband somehow produced a son (I'm sure I had nothing to do with it!) who turned the clock back and became a bona fide, dyed-in-the-wool chassid, much to everyone's surprise. I guess that great paternal grandfather of his from Sighet, a Satmar chassid he was, was determined to redeem at least one of his descendants to the world of chassidus. I think I took it all very well. As I told a friend, worse things shouldn't happen to a Jewish mother.

When we came to Israel, we discovered new dividing lines between Jews. At first, all we were aware of was the "we're the Americans; they're the Israelis" difference. But as we became more Israeli ourselves, the Jewish scene shifted again and the Ashkenazi-Sefardi slant came into view. The old Them-and-Us story with different ways of praying, eating, singing and living. But with the years, these east-west lines have blurred in two interesting — and opposing — directions.

On the one hand, as more and more Israeli-born kids marry across their parents' ethnic lines, our schools, food, music, even some of the customs the average family here practices, are now an international blend of countries and times and communities.

On the other hand, there is a definite strengthening of the ancient and unique Sefardi heritage as the Sefardic community grows, establishes its own educational system, and strengthens its sense of integrity and pride. As another piece of our Jewish kaleidoscope, it is no more foreign to our reality than the Yekkes (German Jews), the Polish Jews, the Hungarians, or the Lithuanians.

When we acquired one lovely daughter-in-law who was 50% Yekke and 50% Buchari, we felt we had passed the Ashkenazi-Sefardi border and left it far behind. Although strictly speaking, the Bucharim aren't Sefardim. They are sort of a border-line case themselves, living as they did on the western side of Russia, or the eastern side of Turkey, depending which side you were standing on. They looked, dressed, sounded and ate eastern, while retaining many western *minhagim,* their own separate *nusach* for praying, and refraining from eating *kitniyos* (lentils) on Pesach — the only "eastern" Jews to do this.

The newest (and perhaps the most unusual to date) division between Jews has become the color of one's clothes. Black Hat/Black Suit versus No Jacket/Knitted Kipa. I wonder where Yosef's striped coat would have fit into this contemporary color-scheme.

Sometimes, even as we progress a step forward, we trip and stumble half a step backward as well. How, for example, did the old chassidic-misnagdic antagonisms — long buried and dead (so we thought) — rise up from the grave to haunt and harass us again? Even when we may opt to retain the richness of difference, superiority and ill will have no place on our agenda. We lost one *Beis Hamikdash* to *sin'as chinam*, and that is more than enough.

※　※　※

There are a few further divisions, old and Divinely ordained, but most aren't operative nowadays. While we still do our best to assign proper identification tags to *Kohanim* (Priests), *Leviim* (Levites), and *Yisraelim* (Israelites), the twelve tribes are no longer recognizable.

Long ago, when the sea split into twelve channels to allow the twelve tribes to pass through, each on its own path; when the tribes walked through the desert, each in its own place; and when the Land of Israel was divided up into twelve sections, one for each tribe, these differences were important. Our own Supreme Court Judge decided that "Separate But Equal" was not only constitutional for the Jews, but beneficial as well. And when the long-awaited day comes and all Jews are gathered together from the four corners of the earth, these Divine distinctions will undoubtedly be reinstated.

☙ ☙ ☙

Until then, I kind of like the way I started out, in a world neatly divided into Jews and gentiles. All the other, internal, divisions only add the spice and keep us from being one homogenized batch. If *Hakadosh Baruch Hu* Himself made billions of people in this world, each one different, then why should all Jews look and sound and think alike?

So we come in different sizes and shades and shapes, all of which make our lives richer and more interesting. We serve G-d and live His Torah in varied, multi-colored ways. Wherever you go, you will find some Jews *davening* one way, some *davening* another; some singing and dressing in one style, and some doing it differently. We celebrate and, when necessary, mourn in distinctly individual tones, with diverse customs, and with varying gastronomical inclinations. Yet we're all from the same basic mold; only the model number is different. And since not every model will automatically fit every Jew, having a good supply of styles on hand is important.

The rule of thumb is: all styles and models are acceptable, as long as they are based on the original, authentic Torah design. (And even if they aren't, don't rush to discard them. A little loving care can often go a long way toward restoring a less than perfect product . . . or person. Especially when the imperfection is due, as it so often is in our time, to ignorance.)

It all goes to show how alive and well the Torah is, from one end of the globe to the other, and how good it feels in a variety of patterns.

❧ ❧ ❧

When the *shtreimlach* and the *spodikim* and the black *yarmulkes* and the knitted *kippot* all meet in our house on *Shabbos* (which they do), we sit back and enjoy. Because in the final reckoning, there really is only that one difference — only one Us and one Them; *Klal Yisrael* on one side and everyone else on the other. For we are the children of Avraham Halvri who stood alone on one side of the river, opposite the rest of the world. He fixed the mold, set the dye and left his stamp on all his many, varying offspring. And no matter how we differ, we are all one.

# Spring Fever and the Glory
# of Growing Things

'm the kind of person who talks in exclamation marks each spring.

"Oh! Look! Leaves! On the trees! And flowers! There! In the weeds! Look at the bird! And the nest!! Ah!!! Smell the honeysuckle! It's absolutely delicious!" And so it is.

My daughter says I'm the only person she ever met who goes around greeting the buds every year. I tell her they deserve to be greeted, every tiny one.

My son remarked that one would think I'd get used to the spring, seeing as how it comes year after year, at the end of every winter. But I don't. How can you get used to a blooming miracle that turns bare, bleak trees into glorious green dancers, paints the landscape in dazzling colors, fills the air with dizzying scents, and stirs up a deep, sweet, aching longing somewhere in the area of the heart? It overwhelms me anew each time the month of *Nissan* comes around.

It seems to me that the female half of the species, privileged as it is with bringing new life into the world, is more in tune with spring, that annual period of rebirth. Perhaps birth of any sort, even the plant variety, speaks more directly to the female soul.

This must be the reason I don't like to throw away cuttings of plants. It's like throwing away good food, or bread. Each cutting is a pregnant plant, ready and willing to put forth shoots and stems and roots and recreate itself in the image of its parent. Who am I to throw away such a wondrous, living organism, leaving it to decay in the garbage? (At least if I left it to decay in a garden, it would recycle itself into some kind of fertilizing agent, and even if it didn't grow, it would not be completely wasted.)

Then there are my cactuses. I like them because tending plants is not my forte, and these take so little care. All I do is water them faithfully, and they reward me by putting forth remarkable flowers in amazing shapes and colors: dainty pointed stars and long hanging bells and wild jungly-looking things. Each one is an incredible creation, and for the life of me, I can't imagine how those fat, prickly, staid-looking parent-plants give birth to such beautiful children!

My first plant experience came from Mr. Kaufman, my fifth grade teacher. Mr. Kaufman was apparently a frustrated scientist who, for some unknown reason, was teaching nine fifth-graders in Chicago's first Hebrew day school. But science's loss was our gain, for he was superb. He opened our eyes and showed us myriads of everyday miracles.

One class project involved growing things with and without fertilizer. Since everyone knows the best things are to be found in their natural state, we went looking for good, natural fertilizer. Fortunately (for our purposes, although I suppose other people might have thought differently), in those days you could still find a few horse-drawn delivery wagons which clattered through Chicago's alleyways, dotting them with manure. So, armed with large coal shovels and metal pails, we trekked through the alleys in search of Nature's gold.

Nature did not disappoint its eager students. My experimental pots produced grass which was lush, thick and green (helped along by the remains of the city's horses), and grass which was sparse, skinny and pale (left hungry and untended, to grow as it would). The benefits of fertilizer were indelibly imprinted on my young mind.

But the most exciting class project was our compost pile. The class spent weeks collecting fallen leaves and garbage. In the garage behind the schoolyard, we built our own personal garbage dump, watered it (it had to be kept damp), covered it (it had to be kept dark), turned it this way and that (it had to be aired) and we watched as another miracle took place under our very eyes (and noses). Dirty, smelly wastes turned into odorless, organic, life-giving fertilizer which we then divided up among the students for their own gardens.

It was a wonderful experience, and to this day, whenever I see someone burning leaves, I think of Mr. Kaufman. For him, burning leaves was *baal tashchis* — a wasteful sin. Dead leaves were not dead at all; they were a concentrated form of fertilizer, a catalyst for rich, new life.

And for me, the smell of manure is still the smell of growing things. With the help of Chicago's unknowing horses, I grew carrots, miniature tomatoes, and a few other vegetables I can't remember. I will admit, that thrilled as I was with the food I was raising, I still wondered about the effect of the manure on my product. Manure on flower beds was one thing, but for food? Was it sufficiently sterilized? But fortified with faith in G-d's agricultural wisdom, we ate the produce, and if there were any negative results, they're since forgotten.

My mother, *z"l*, was a great grower of things. When we think of her plant prowess, it's the tomato riot that immediately comes to mind. During one of her visits to us in Israel, before she herself moved here, we were living in a small, rural area. While throwing out the garbage one day, a tomato must have fallen onto the ground next to the garbage can and taken root.

Always the first to spy signs of new life, my mother reported the tiny plant and enlisted the family for immediate action. The area was roped off, the garbage can moved, and a daily watering schedule set up. The plant, realizing it had fallen into a virtual Garden of Eden, thrived. In short time, it was putting forth hard green balls which turned into big, soft, juicy, red tomatoes.

That amazing plant, that cast-off piece of refuse which didn't even make it to the garbage pail, kept us (and the neighbors) in tomatoes for a full two months. Everyone in the *yishuv* came by to see it. By now tall, six feet high and supported by an intricate framework of sticks and broom handles, it stood in a place of honor, rivaled only by the old olive tree in our backyard.

Each morning the children ran out to see what new fruit had come forth. They counted and recounted the tomatoes, monitoring them for signs of ripeness. And woe unto any foolish passerby who unthinkingly yanked one off without permission!

Like all living things, its glory came to an end, and as the summer waned, our tomato plant waned along with it, until it finally returned unto the dirt from which it had sprung. We had been grateful for its existence, and mourned its demise.

Wouldn't it be wonderful if a table (or bed or window or radio) could reproduce and create a copy of itself like that tomato plant? And wouldn't it be nice if one pair of shoes could turn into two like my cactuses do? Unfortunately, they can't. This particular trick was reserved only for living, growing things. One donkey plus mate produces a third. A cow, with a little help from a bull, makes a similar copy. A bed or table or radio has only a single, solitary existence and when its days are over, that's the end of that.

In earlier times, people prized living things. Horses, donkeys and cows were real property — the only kind of asset which multiplied indefinitely with a minimum of care. In our times, especially in the urban environment in which most of us live, we tend to forget this, often valuing inanimate objects above living ones.

So if you haven't done so until now, turn an awed eye on the next growing thing you encounter. It may turn into a loaf of bread to nourish and keep you alive; it may become a blazing mass of red and orange and purple flowers to make the world more beautiful and give you pleasure. It may end up in a pill to cure you of some illness, or as a blouse or skirt to wear. (Did you ever see a cotton ball? An amazing thing if ever there was one!)

And where does it all stem from? From the dirt we walk on, the stones beneath our feet, from the inert, lifeless minerals in the ground. From these lowly sources are we nourished and enabled to live and thrive and multiply.

Amazing, isn't it? It's enough to make you talk in biological exclamation marks all year long.

# It Takes All Kinds

niformity is not a human characteristic. Every human being is a unique personality which represents a unique, personal world. *Chazal* said, "He who saves a single Jewish life is considered as having saved the entire world," for each and every human being is cast in a different mold; each is special, unmatched, and precious. Not only physically, but every other way as well. "Just as their faces are all different, so are their ideas never the same."

We may all trace our lineage back to one common ancestor, but the human scene diversified soon after his appearance. Eventually, seventy nations represented the spectrum of human society, and even G-d's One Nation was divided up into twelve tribes, each with its own individual "path to the Divine."

So why do we lump people together into groups, or package them in neat, orderly stacks as though they were boxes of food in the supermarket? Why do we seem to feel more secure when each type or subdivision is immediately recognizable? Perhaps it's the desire to find some order in a confusing, multifaceted world. Or an innate longing to reunite with the supreme simplicity of the primordial One.

Whatever the reason, it doesn't work. Not only that, it causes untold tension and suffering. For the world is full of stubborn people who refuse to be categorized, and if they are, they refuse to stay put in whichever category we have placed them.

These "unboxable" people are often among the brightest, the most interesting, the most valuable treasures we possess. And by denying their diversity, we lose their talents, and often their hearts.

Take our children, for example. Many of our kids are misfits in rigid school systems. They are perfectly normal kids — likable, capable, intelligent and well adjusted. They just don't necessarily fit into the highly structured beehives we call schools. And when they are assigned to a class nonetheless, and made to sit still, they don't seem to learn much — especially the boys, who are subjected to the rigors of learning *gemara* at an early age and who are expected to succeed, but who often don't. Examples abound.

One bright and charming seventh grader I know of was considered a mediocre student. He was enrolled in an ambitious, scholarly institution and one of the better *rebbes* was his teacher. But while he wasn't making any trouble, he wasn't making any progress either. His mother, who knew a bright kid when she saw one, went to speak to his *rebbe.*

"Why," she asked, "doesn't my son learn with a bit of enthusiasm? Why does he just sit here for six or seven hours a day looking out the window?" (It was springtime. . ...)

"Ah," lamented the teacher, "I wish I knew. It's a pity, too, because he's a bright lad. But if I want to get anywhere with the really good learners, I have no time to worry about the dreamers."

She changed her son's school and within three weeks he was at the head of his new class, raring to go, devouring every word.

What can one learn from this? Was the first *rebbe* poor? No. Was the first class too hard? No. Was the second school better? Probably not. But in the second school, the *rebbe* found time for the dreamers, thus waking up many of the Sleeping Beauties (or, in this case, Princes) who had been given up as lost causes before.

Another child, the son of a good friend, read everything he could get his hands on — history, geography, politics, math. He just couldn't seem to get his hands — or his mind — on *gemara*. He went through twelve years as a Talmudic dud (although a great student in everything else), and it took many years for him to discover that it was not Jewish learning he so disliked; it was the feeling of failure he had acquired in Jewish education. Having somehow missed the train in that first or second year of *gemara*, he watched with resignation as his classmates sped forever forward, leaving him ever further behind.

And I cannot forget the ten-year old whose parents took him for psychological testing because he was doing so poorly in class. The psychologist, after an hour or two with the child, came out to speak to mom and dad.

"Why did you bring this kid to me?" he asked. "He's perfectly normal, charming, intelligent, capable and talented, with a higher than normal I.Q.! He's just not a theoretical learner. Give him a concrete problem to solve or something to fix and he'll do wonders. If you owned a farm or a garage or a business, instead of expecting your son to be a scholar, you'd be delighted with him!"

Which was true. But the boy's family and his school system

were both programmed to produce only Jewish scholars, not Torah-true mechanics or technicians or farm hands or businessmen. No one had thought of providing for bright, talented, "practical" Jewish children. It took a special tutor and a long time to make the *gemara* more "concrete" for this boy, and I suspect that the rest of his class could have benefited from a bit of concrete teaching as well.

Because our school systems are not always oriented towards these fine, normal, but not-always-scholarly kids (and there are thousands of them), we lose many. They are lost to the world of *talmidei chachamim,* and sometimes even to the world of good *balabatim*. For no child (and no adult) wants to remain in a framework where his particular talents are not encouraged or allowed to develop; no one wants to spend years in a milieu which labels him "unsatisfactory."

❧ ❧ ❧

One of my fantasies has long been to start a school for these boys. (I'm sure girls could use one, too, but in our house, where the male offspring far outnumbered the females, my mind usually runs along masculine lines.) Mine would not be a school for slow learners or learning disabled children (now that we finally have schools for these kids). Nor would it be a school for geniuses and budding scholars — (the kind of students most other Jewish schools try to attract).

My school would be for the average, bright, active, not-always-aching-to-learn kid; the one who has nothing wrong with him, does most things right most of the time, but who is not turned on by our present teaching methods. The one who goes through twelve years of Jewish schooling and still comes out less than delighted with *gemara*. Which is a pity and a loss if ever there was one.

In my school, the *rebbes* would worry about this average kid, aiming to reach him and kindle his particular soul-spark so that he, too, could soar. And if the methods needed proved to be slightly irregular, then so be it.

❦ ❦ ❦

It's not just our school system which is rough on individuals. It's our ideas of how people should dress or speak; what they should eat or read; how they should decorate their homes and what they may do for a living. Certain ways of doing things are always wrong, and some are always right, but within the "rights," there is a broad range of possibilities. Not everyone has to think and look and act alike, and if we think they do, then we are limiting the great scope of expression which G-d has granted to man.

One exceptionally talented woman, a convert of long standing, told me that she had a pair of earth-shoes she had packed away, afraid to wear them for fear of what "people would say." It took twelve years for her to say "I don't care what people will say," and wear her comfortable-but-not-too-attractive shoes. Together with her shoes, she had hidden away many marvelous gifts she could have shared with the community. Unfortunately, she felt that these too would mark her as "different." They may have. After all, how many exceptionally gifted people are just like everyone else? But because we do not always take kindly to "differences," we were denied the beauty and joy she could have brought us.

❦ ❦ ❦

"Square," regular people are indispensable. They keep our world spinning and we cannot possibly manage without them. Many of our most important people are "square" — perfect right angles on all four sides. Changing even one degree would ruin their entire style and disposition and prevent them from fulfilling their vital jobs.

But when the world presents us with round boxes to fill (as

it inevitably does), we need round people to do the job. Ditto for triangles, or ovals or parallelograms.

One of the most precious qualities which the influx of *baaley teshuvah* has brought to us (and they bring at least as much as they receive) is a heightened sense of individuality. Coming as they do from different places, professions and backgrounds, they inject an additional measure of hetero-geneity into our social setting, reminding us that not all people look, sound, think or act alike.

It's a healthy addition to the Jewish scene. May they — and we — proliferate!

# Abi Gezunt! It's Only Warts

he quest for health is never ending, the topic never exhausted. In my younger days I always smiled indulgently at the elderly people who were forever peppering their conversations with "*abi gezunt* — as long as we are healthy," or "*zeit mir gezunt* — be well." Then as I became a little older myself (it happens to everyone), I found that references to health were creeping into my own conversations, at an alarming rate. Obviously, we are concerned with our health. And just as obviously, we are not sure what to do about it.

Acupuncture, yoga, shiatsu? Pain killers, antibiotics, tranquilizers? Hormones, vitamins, health foods? The possible treatments for any given ailment are endless. Yet, precisely because so much pharmaceutical help is available, we often overlook the body's own incredible power to heal itself.

In his book, *The Medusa and the Snail*, Dr. Lewis Thomas

wrote about an ancient human affliction — warts. Experiments had proved that warts could be removed by hypnosis. In other words, by implanting a thought (in this instance, the command to rid the body of the wart) in the patient's brain, the body understood exactly what had to be done. It accepted the command and went on to produce the complex chemical-hormonal mixture necessary to displace the unwanted growth.

Please note that no one told the brain which chemicals and hormones to produce, in which quantities, where to send them, or at which intervals. That's because doctors simply don't know the answers to these questions. Tom Sawyer, I believe, used a frog or a toad to remove warts. Other than cutting or burning the wart off, doctors today don't do much better. Yet the brain, just by being instructed to knock that wart off, goes ahead, all on its own and without the benefit of a college degree, and does the job!

I found the implications of this information absolutely overwhelming. Somehow, locked into the little gray cells inside our skull, G-d has implanted sophisticated medical information which works even without our knowledge. All we have to do is press the correct button and the entire marvelous system turns on, all by itself. Imagine — every human being equipped with his or her own free, internal, computerized hospital complete with pharmaceutical factory! It was mind-boggling.

❦ ❦ ❦

Shortly after reading this article, I came upon another piece of intriguing information. After having been under unusually severe tension for several years, a man found himself on the brink of a nervous breakdown. He was experiencing strange visions and was positive that the soul of another person had been placed into the body of his former self.

His doctor explained that as a result of the severe tension he had experienced, certain chemical and hormonal imbalances were caused in his nervous system, leading to the temporary disintegration of his personality. The doctor had suggested strong drugs to reinstate the normal body balance, but when the patient objected to taking medicine, a regime of complete rest and relaxation, far removed from the source of the tension, had been prescribed. After prolonged care, the patient regained his own personality and normalcy.

I thought about that for a while. To put it very simply, it meant that if the world makes us crazy (which it often does), a little peace and quiet can do wonders. We've all heard this before, of course, but I had never heard of such a severe illness and such a complete cure. And without drugs. Nowadays, we don't have time for slow cures. Instead of allowing the body's marvelous, built-in resources to effect their own slow, natural healing, we prefer a bottle of pills and z'bang (as they say in Hebrew slang) — instant health is on its way.

❧   ❧   ❧

It is said that a person who believes he is well, tends to remain well; one who is happy, tends to shed illnesses more quickly and easily; one who believes that the cold symptoms he has contracted will not develop into a cold, tends not to develop a cold.

This seems to imply that we have a very definite measure of control over our health simply by maintaining a happy, positive attitude towards life. This information was so exciting and brimming with promise that I had trouble digesting it.

Then, at a *shiur* in the Book of Daniel, we came across something which helped my "digestion." Instead of the elaborate, gourmet food which Nevuchadnezer had prepared for his young captives, Daniel and his Jewish friends requested and received plain, inexpensive *zer'onim* (a form of lentils) to eat. Not only were they satisfied and well nourished, but they felt great and looked better than all the lads who ate the more superior, non-kosher fare.

One of the commentaries explains that if we eat food which we want and like, even if it has less food value, the body digests it more fully and it is ultimately more nourishing and healthier.

※ ※ ※

Does all of this mean that the body has a way of deriving more — or less — nutrients from food, depending on the attitude of the eater? Does it perhaps explain why so many unfortunate things seem to happen to people who feel unfortunate, while happier people have more positive experiences? (It doesn't always work that way, of course, but some people do seem more adept at the art of living.)

If it's true, what a priceless gift it is! By just thinking positively, we can somehow revolutionize our lives, making them better, happier, richer in human experiences, and healthier!

Our family physician seems to agree. He never says "goodbye." He always sends his patients away with a resounding "*tihiyu semeychim* — be happy." It took me several years to realize that this wasn't just a linguistic idiosyncrasy; it was a piece of serious medical advice.

Many of us fritter away precious energy during our lifetimes, trying to redesign the world. If only we could learn to relax, be satisfied, be happy, and trust in G-d to do His job, we could get on with ours, and enjoy a larger measure of success while we're at it. And the energy we saved in the process could then be put to better use, helping our bodies perform in the magnificent manner for which they were originally programmed.

There is no doubt that the human body possesses great powers and strengths which modern medicine barely suspects, let alone comprehends. If only we work with it, instead of against it — combining faith and joy and a little common sense — we will be royally rewarded.

So relax, be happy, and *abi gezunt!*

# The Financial Scene

ONEY. What a powerful, all-pervading word in our vocabulary. Like air, sun, sleep and water, money seems to be one of the basic givens in the world. But unlike air, sun, sleep and water which are universal and (more or less) free, money seems to be a difficult-to-acquire ingredient which takes up a good deal of our time and energy. So much so, that one sometimes wonders if it's worth the effort.

For money isn't always everything it's cracked up to be. It may smooth a lot of bumps in the roads we travel, but it can also disguise imperfections and serious faults which need fixing. It can also confuse us into thinking that our personal value is determined by the size of our bank account, or our debts, or our credit rating — an outrageous, un-Jewish error if ever there was one.

Credit ratings have almost displaced bank accounts as necessities in life. In our era of "plastic money" when credit cards are the magic ticket to the wonderworld of stores and acquiring things, many kids (big people, too) no longer even know the names of the presidents whose pictures grace the green bills which pay their way. And no wonder. In order to pay with green bills, you have to own some; but with those magic plastic cards, you just buy-now-pay-later. Pull them out of your pocket or purse, scribble a signature of sorts, and instant gratification is yours with the bills a long month away. They are a *yetzer hara's* dream.

When we were kids, our father refused to let us buy on credit. "When there's money in your pocket, you'll find what to buy" was his motto. It seemed fair and sensible, for the idea of "owing" was repulsive. Many years later in Israel, our first large purchase was cabinets for our small kitchen. We gave the carpenter ten post-dated checks and for the next ten months I had this nagging feeling that I was in the clutches of Debt. When the last check was finally canceled, it was a day of Release and Redemption. Debt had been banished (for the time being).

Not only were there no credit cards in our youth; there were no free gimmicks in our family either. If it was for free, it was suspect. To this day, I tend to look down upon and shy away from freebies. If the supermarket gives a bonus buy, I know they are overcharging on some other product to pay for it, and it spoils any joy the free gift might bring. *Soney matanos yichyeh* — He who hates gifts will enjoy the gift of life. It was my father's credo and he passed it faithfully down.

On the other hand, there's no point in being a Scrooge. Money is a tool for living, and if it expedites things, use it. A cousin once spent two hours driving across town to buy tuna-fish at bargain prices thus saving, I believe it was, $3.30 on ten cans. But when I took a cab for eight dollars to save myself an hour ride on three buses on a freezing, snowy day, she accused me of being a spendthrift. I'd rather be a spendthrift with money than with my precious time any day. Money comes and goes (although the going is usually quicker than the coming), but time, once gone, never returns.

They say that most marital problems center around the subject of money — too much of it (hard to imagine as a problem, but evidently for some, it is); too little of it; how it should be spent; when; and by whom. Obviously, dealing with money is serious business, even in the privacy of one's home.

It can be annoying, too, especially in the context of never-ending requests by the younger generation. If they had to earn it, we think, they'd appreciate it more. Yet, good Jewish parents that we are, we don't really want them spending the precious years of their youth worrying about and working for money. There are other, more important things they should be doing while they can.

This seems to be a very Jewish attitude. The differences in what parents think they "owe" their children are a fascinating study in cultural values. Jewish parents — and the more observant they are, the more this seems to be true — tend to "help" their children far more and much longer than other parents. This can, of course, result in highly spoiled kids. It can also result in grateful, responsible ones, aware of the fact that money "doesn't grow on trees," and thankful for their parents' efforts. Please G-d, they, in turn, will do the same for their offspring.

❦ ❦ ❦

Every society has rules which govern its relationship to money, and making a big deal about small sums is considered vaguely impolite, at least in the West. The Middle East is a different story, however, and in the haggling manner of the local marketplace, I once argued with a storekeeper about the cost of an item which I knew for a fact was overpriced.

"Aren't you ashamed," the storekeeper asked me angrily, "a

respectable woman like you, arguing with me over such a paltry sum?"

For a moment, I was embarrassed. Then I started to laugh.

"And aren't you ashamed," I retorted, "a respectable man like you, arguing with a customer over such a paltry sum?"

I don't mind overpaying a bit if there's a reason for it (a more convenient place to shop, a nicer storekeeper, someone who I know needs the money more than I do), but all things being equal, my penny is as dear to me as the next fellow's is to him.

One lady told me the story of a taxi ride with a rude driver whom she did not feel like tipping. When her bill came to $4.95, she handed him a five dollar bill and said stonily, "Keep the change." The angry driver took a nickel, threw it out the window, and told her to keep it herself.

She didn't hesitate for a second. With her usual aplomb, she flashed him a winning smile and said, "Why, thank you!" She picked up the coin and marched triumphantly away.

"I wouldn't have had the nerve to do that," I mumbled. "I would just have disappeared fast."

"And wasted a good nickel?" she answered. "What for?"

What for indeed? The Torah says, "You shall love *Hashem*, your G-d, with all your heart, all your soul and all your might." *Rashi* explains that "might" means money, and he knew what he was talking about. Our money rates right up there after our hearts and souls, perhaps because money represents precious time and hard effort, the raw ingredients of life itself. You might sum it up by saying "Money is Time," instead of "Time is money."

Money is something else too. Sometimes, all the time and effort in the world do not suffice to fill our coffers. In the last reckoning, whatever we own or earn is a personal loan from the Director of the World Bank, and we are expected to invest and utilize it in accordance with His Divine instructions. If we use it well, remembering that it is only a temporary deposit in our account, the interest earned will be ours to keep. If we are guilty of misuse, appropriating our assets solely for our own personal needs and desires, we will be held accountable.

"Money talks." Even attitudes about money talk, telling us much about the people who hold them. During a period of rampant inflation in Israel in the 1980's, prices changed from day to day. As they rocketed sky high, the value of the shekel plummeted down low. Things were chaotic in the extreme.

In the midst of all this economic confusion, a good friend was visited by his relatives from abroad. They were well-established people, the type who have their money safely invested and their financial affairs under tight control.

"How do you manage?" they asked, knowing that our friend's profession was hardly lucrative and that even in the best of times, his salary was average in the extreme. "How can you get through the month? How can you pay your bills in such a crazy situation?"

"Well, I'm not quite sure, but we manage," he answered.

"Look," they said, "we're close relatives — and friends! Tell us the truth. How do you do it?"

He hemmed and hawed, wondering how one explains the unexplainable.

"Well, you see, it's like this. Firstly, we don't buy all that much. And last week I got a refund of a few hundred shekel from a tax bill we overpaid two years ago. There's also a little extra money that comes in for a vacation bonus in August. We didn't use the money for vacation, but it's very handy for other things. And of course, like everybody else, we have a big overdraft with the bank. But they don't bounce our checks. They know we won't run away."

"But those are only stopgap solutions!" they said. "All those things together will tide you over for a month or two. Then what happens?"

What happens? Now *that* was an easy question to answer! "*Hashem ya'azor* — G-d will help!" he said promptly. He meant it too.

They shook their heads in disbelief, probably suspecting that he was moonlighting or had a neat pile stashed away somewhere. But he didn't. And G-d did help. No one starved; no one slept in the streets; no one suffered (unless you call the lack of a vacation or new clothing suffering). The economy eventually calmed down; a raise was forthcoming; and the overdraft was reduced, if not fully covered. And life went on. *Baruch Hashem yom yom* — thank G-d for each and every day.

It's hard to explain such a seemingly lackadaisical attitude to financially oriented people, but perhaps it's not lackadaisical at all. Money, like everything else, is a gift. We work hard and do the best we can, always aiming to give (and, if possible, to get) full value. Then we hope and pray for the best.

Quick or easy money is not a Jewish concept; giving full value is. The Torah tells us that Chanoch, who was the seventh generation after Adam, "walked with G-d." The *Midrash* says that Chanoch was a cobbler who, with every stitch he sewed, achieved "mystical unions" with his Creator. Rabbi Yisrael Salanter, *zt"l*, explained that it is forbidden to engage in mystical pursuits in the midst of doing hired labor. Therefore, Chanoch's "unions" were:

> "...nothing more or less than the concentration he lavished on each and every stitch to ensure that it would be good and strong and that the shoes he was making would be a good pair, giving the maximum pleasure and benefit to whoever would wear them... His taking would never exceed the value of the work he was doing."
>
> (*Strive for Truth*, Rabbi Eliyahu E. Dessler)

It's called "*yashrus*" — integrity. It means being a *mentsh*, and, when all is said and done, having *bitachon*. And we pray that our kids will learn it too, even if, as good Jewish parents, we do tend to indulge them a bit.

# A Time For All Things

*Everything has its season, and there is a time for everything under the heavens.*
*(Koheles 3:1)*

hat Koheles didn't mention is that there are also different kinds of time in which to do all the many things we have to do. There is, for example, what I call Prime Time. These are the good hours in the morning (or in the afternoon or evening, depending on your own individual biological clock, or before the kids are expected home from school). This is when you have a few fresh, empty hours to get something important done. It's time you garner and protect, time you don't want to fritter away on phone calls or something dumb. Because if you lose this Prime Time (thereby turning it into Wasted or Lost Time), you may not find it again for days or weeks. Or even months.

The opposite of Prime Time is Squeeze-In Time. This is small amounts of time, not enough for anything major. Squeeze-In-Time is usually filled with simple, small, willing-to-be-squashed-into-extra-time items. Things like phone calls, scrubbing a particular pot, or potting a particular plant. I write letters in Squeeze-In Time, although a good friend of mine says that for her, letter writing is a Prime Time item. On the other hand, she pays her bills and balances her checkbook in Squeeze-In Time, while for me, those are Prime Time activities par excellence.

There is Opportune Time you don't want to let slip by, and Time-Out to catch your breath. There is Wartime and Peacetime and all sorts of unclear times in between. There is Worktime and Playtime and Time-for-a-Nap. And if Time is Money, don't we all wish we could collect the world's (or our own!) wasted minutes each day and deposit them in a timely bundle in some celestial savings account!

For an infant or small child, Immediacy is the name of the game. Whatever a child wants, he wants Now. Young People's Time, on the other hand, tends to be somewhat schizophrenic. Although it has progressed beyond the pressing immediacy of the infant's Now, it still tends to treat the Present as the only decent time in which to fulfill all one's needs and desires, while relegating responsibilities to some vague era in the distant future.

How long is time? Is an hour, a week, a year considered long, or short? The answer is neither. Time condenses and expands. An hour of pain is a long hour indeed, while an hour of pleasure disappears before we know it. When life is dull, time drags; when it's interesting and full, time flies.

One's view of time also changes with age. Ask a kid how long a year is. The answer will inevitably be: long. Any normal adult will tell you most years are over shortly after they begin.

❈ ❈ ❈

Nothing reminds man of his own mortality more than Time. One of the most oft-repeated expressions in western civilization is "There's no time." Why could G-d not have been more generous with us, allotting us more time, like in the good old days, when Adam and Chavah and Mesushelach and all their relatives lived long, long years on this earth? Frail creatures that we are, we spend three quarters of our lives just learning the rules and setting things up before we begin to appreciate and enjoy. What a pity we have to leave it all so soon!

Our sages explained long ago why G-d shortened the life of man: the sparsity of our years is precisely the reason we value them. Only the very young or the very foolish can convince themselves that they are immortal actors on the stage of life. And even if the foolish don't get any wiser, the young always get older, thus helping man to keep his priorities in proper working order.

And when we consider the damage and sorrow man often manages to inflict even during a short lifetime, one wonders what he might do with a few hundred more years at his disposal. When viewed in this light, seventy-plus years are years enough.

Time highlights the difference between the Creator and the created. G-d is timeless, eternal, without beginning and without end. But we small creatures are granted only a finite piece of time, usually spent running around and taking care of things. Even the time allotted us is never completely at our disposal, for our yesterdays are already gone and our tomorrows, despite all of our planning and arranging, are an unknown.

This, of course, is why the only sensible thing to do is to gratefully accept each moment as it comes — savoring it, filling it with Torah, *mitzvos,* love and good deeds, and treating it like the priceless jewel it is. At least then we can say that our time was well spent.

# Just Passing Through

## Memory Lane

The Torah commands us, time and time again, to "remember" — the Sabbath; the Exodus from Egypt; the Giving of the Torah; the evil Amalek. Even the beginning of our year is a Day of Remembrance. To remember means to be a part of something, to have a place in the larger scheme of things. Remembering means connection with a past, and a past implies a future. Our memories, both personal and collective, form the basis of our identity. They tell us who we are, which is why we are commanded to keep our collective, national memory in good order.

Our personal memories, however, are a different story. They tend to get lost in the shuffle of everyday affairs. Yet under the influence of hypnosis even these memories can be recalled. Stored carefully away in our brain, under layer upon layer of more recent events, the old memories are all faithfully recorded and retained.

If, in the normal course of events, we forget so much, there's undoubtedly an important reason why. Perhaps if we were able to live too fully and freely in the past, the business of living in the present would suffer. Perhaps it's not really necessary to remember everything; and most of us would agree that some things are best forgotten. Still, it would be nice to recall some of the better things in clearer detail.

Be that as it may, whatever memories we retain are something to be thankful for. A good memory brings you a face long unseen, a voice long unheard, and sights and smells long forgotten. It gives you a return ticket to a performance you may wish to experience again. How empty and poor our lives would be if we only had the present to keep us company, but not the past!

The young tend to look forward in time; but the older we grow, the more there is to see when we look back. May our memories be happy, rich and heartwarming ones.

# A World of People

grew up in a warm, friendly, loving world. (Many years later, in a college English course, the class was reading a novel about a teenager and his dissonant, conflicted, unhappy world. When asked whether it sounded familiar to me or not, all I could say was I couldn't possibly imagine where *he* grew up!)

The West Side of Chicago in those days was a Jewish neighborhood par excellence, despite the presence of Poles, Italians and other peoples. Mostly, it was a family neighborhood where a fifteen-minute walk in any direction would take us to one of two grandmothers, many aunts and uncles, and scores of cousins.

*Pesach Sedarim* were crowded, noisy affairs; *Tashlich* was a gala march among thousands of people to a lagoon two miles away. In the summer, our annual family picnic, always well attended by second and third and fourth cousins from the *landsmanschaft* club, filled the forest preserves; and all through the seasons, friends and cousins played on the sidewalks, in the backyards, on the porches — ball, rope, jacks, hopscotch, checkers, hide-and-seek.

The highlight of the year was the period of the *Yamim Noraim*, the High Holidays. Amidst a flurry of new clothing and the smells of cakes and gefilte fish and other gastronomic delights, we made our way to shul. In those days Chicago's two boulevards boasted almost twenty imposing synagogues — tall, elaborate affairs with splendid, majestic doorways, stately marble staircases, and inspiring *aroney-kodesh* filled with dozens of *sifrey Torah*. The competition between *chazzanim* during the holidays was fierce.

Our *shul*, Kehillas Yaakov, was a medium-large building with gold-colored handrails, thick oak furniture and carpeted steps and floors. The halls were shiny marble, and both the *bimah* and the *aron* were covered with thick, purple velvet. As a child, I was sure the decor was a detailed copy of the *Beis Hamikdash* itself.

My father and uncles had permanent seats in the second or third row, and one uncle, president of the shul, sat on the *bimah*. My young *davening* days were spent either Downstairs next to my father (but with my own *siddur* or *machzor!*) or Upstairs in the women's gallery, next to my bubby (the Queen of Upstairs), my mother and my aunts. Each place had its own delights to offer.

Upstairs was the best place to watch our *chazzan*. Year after year, he sang in our shul. Even when he became blind, he continued to *daven* — all of Rosh Hashanah and Yom Kippur — by heart. To this day, I hum his *niggunim* when we reach the prayer *Unesaneh Tokef*.

The high point of the holidays for the children was Simchas Torah. Unconcerned with fire hazards, we marched proudly to shul with our flags, topped with apples, topped with candles which we lit with abandon once inside the shul. Our fiery *hakafos* warmed the hearts of all viewers (and probably made them nervous, too, but I was blissfully unaware of that.)

The following morning climaxed with the "young boys' *aliyah*" — the last of the many *aliyos* on *Simchas Torah,* when all the minor set was gathered up under a great *tallis* to make a communal *brachah.* They rushed into the shul en masse from their games in the park across the street, determined not to miss "their" turn. I had no doubt that the blessing made upon the children descended in a straight line from *Hakadosh Baruch Hu* Himself.

❀ ❀ ❀

The West Side boasted more than synagogues. It had hundreds of stores, each one with its own particular sights and smells (and sometimes tastes). Shopping was a regular kaleidoscope of consumer delights.

In addition to fruits and vegetables, the vegetable man and his wife also sold eggs (which he drank raw if they broke); the fish store had live fish and smelled of the sea; the grocery store was lined with wonderful wooden barrels full of pickles and spices; the butcher with his meat cleaver and his bloodied apron was a man to be feared.

❀ ❀ ❀

People came to the house more frequently in those days. Doctors made home visits; the milkman was a good family friend; janitors came and went. The mailman would stop by to say hello; the Fuller Brush man brought his wares up the back stairs into the kitchen; and once a month, dusty coal-men dumped mountains of black coal into the yard and proceeded to shovel it down the chute into the basement.

Itinerant *meshulachim* also came and went. Interesting people who sat in the kitchen or front room (depending on whether they came in the morning when my mother was home, or at night when my father greeted them). They came from faraway cities and countries — even Palestine! — drank tea, and spoke mostly in Yiddish. They were an International Jewish Exchange where we heard first-hand news of *Klal Yisrael*. I had my favorites (usually elderly) whom I waited for and greeted personally.

After The War ("The War" always meant World War II) came the refugees. They were the people who had actually lived through the unbelievable stories we had been hearing; the ones who had numbers tattooed on their arms. One was careful what one said in their presence, careful so as not to hurt or probe or embarrass.

Our upstairs neighbor rented a room to a refugee family and I would go up to play with their little daughter. She was a pitifully thin little girl with great brown eyes, and her mother was always fighting to feed her soup plates full of a dreadful, gray porridge. I wondered why she didn't cook something more appetizing, not realizing, in my childish innocence, that more appetizing food might have cost more than this family could afford. But I did my best to help, telling the little girl stories in my broken Yiddish ("The Three Bears" was my crowning glory) as I ladled spoonfuls of cereal down her throat.

Lastly, there were the neighbors. The Jewish ones on the block were all sort of extended family; the gentiles provided the background against which our Jewish stage was set. Their presence was a constant reminder that despite its warm, homey flavor, Chicago was still only another *galus*.

Like all *galuyos*, this one too came to an end. The neighborhood changed; the Jews all moved away. Today, the majestic synagogues along the boulevards have turned into churches, public schools, community centers — their large Magen Davids torn down, their enormous *mezuzos* removed, their grand Hebrew lettering cemented over. They are like the old cemetery where my grandparents are buried. But in my memory, they are still alive.

# Just Like Mom

s we become parents and grow a little older, we discover — often to our amazement — how very like our parents we have become. Or always were. Perhaps we were so busy trying to be different and independent when we were younger that we just never noticed.

But there's no getting away from it. Every time you open your mouth, there's your mother or father talking right out of it; using the same expressions, too. I even hear my parents when my *children* talk! It sets me to wondering. Did my bubby sound the same way? I don't remember. And what about my great-grandmother? Not having reached the shores of America, she didn't know any English. But surely some of her verbal style crossed the sea with her daughters? How did it get translated?

I once read about a woman who gave her children strawberries whenever they were sad. When asked why, she thought a moment and said, "Because that's what my mother did." She checked it out a bit further and discovered that her grandmother had done the same. Her family was from cold, northern Sweden where strawberries could only have been a rarity. That being the case, perhaps their appearance was a cause for rejoicing, after which strawberries became, in her clan at least, a cure for sorrow. Such are the humble beginnings of great family customs.

Offhand, I can't think of too many private family customs among my own relatives. Perhaps as Jews, they moved around too often for any to develop. But I was privileged to see two generations of joyous women, living each day to the fullest.

My Bubby Blima, *z"l*, came to America as a young girl of twelve or thirteen. She traveled alone to join her two elder brothers and a sister in Indianapolis. It was the last time she ever saw her parents, who never did make it to the *goldine medinah*. Despite a life of hardship and often poverty, she was a regal lady whose breeding shone through, even during the poor years (and there were many). Widowed and left with three small children in the days when there was no way for a woman to make a living, she soon remarried; her new husband came with an additional six children as his contribution to the "dowry." Shortly after their marriage, they completed their "*minyan*," raising all ten children through the Great Depression (and through many other difficulties). But wherever she went, my bubby carried with her the seeds of joy, and whenever I think of her, I smile.

Like her mother before her, my mother accepted life as a great gift, a challenge, something to shape and improve and treasure. She embraced each day, then rolled up her sleeves and went to work to see how she could best fill it.

A child of the Depression, she was unable to continue her

education past high school, but her spirit was undaunted. She had a flair for life which led her to investigate — music, people, sports, crafts. Hungry and eager to learn, she read. Denied any sort of a scholarly Jewish education (girls didn't get any outside the house in those days), she learned how to read and write and *daven* and speak Hebrew after she was married.

Perhaps because of her own lack of formal Jewish schooling, she and my father registered their daughters in Chicago's first fledgling Hebrew day school in the days when it was not a popular thing to do. (For years, the relatives kept saying "They'll never learn how to speak English or how to get along with *goyim!*") Then, seeing how precarious an institution the school was, she became the president of the P.T.A. for long, hard, work-filled years.

Broken furnaces, unpaid bills, teachers' salaries; working in the office, organizing affairs, raising money; writing ads, pleading for aid from the neighborhood alderman and discussing curriculum problems with the principal — nothing was too difficult; nothing was impossible.

In those days, many of our *rebbeim* came from Europe and their knowledge of English was sparse, if not nonexistent. Sparse or nonexistent was also the way you could describe our grasp of Yiddish. But we *teiched* in Yiddish (even though we barely understood what we were saying) because the teachers would not or could not teach in English. Everyone was unhappy with the situation, but no one knew what to do.

So my mother approached the principal and the rabbis, and in her Americanized Yiddish, and with her usual grace and goodwill and *cheyn,* she convinced the teachers to give English a chance. To their great surprise, they managed, and everyone was pleased with the results.

When she finally decided to "retire" from the school, I pleaded with her to wait until my graduation so that she, as president of the P.T.A., would be the one to hand me my diploma at the ceremony. She did, and I was proud.

❀　❀　❀

My mother enjoyed people, and she opened the doors of her home wide. The house was always full; as was the fridge — with homemade foods, cookies, pies and cakes, expertly done, beautiful to look at and delicious to eat. While others cooked because cooking was a necessity, she cooked like an artist. It was a creative labor of love.

Blessed with "golden hands," she tried everything at least once, just to see if it could be done. It usually could. The results of her efforts still hang on our walls, decorate our tables and clothe her daughters and granddaughters. I remember great vegetable bouquets she carved, plays and songs she wrote, costumes she put together; she tried her hand at designing, knitting, embroidering — everything but sewing, which may explain my own lack of enthusiasm for that particular craft.

Hospitable and outgoing, she was a great party giver. Birthday parties, graduation parties, anniversary parties, *simchahs,* organizational affairs, money-raising events. Hers were lavish, lovely, delicious affairs. Each was a one-woman job, planned, orchestrated and executed by her, from beginning to end, right down to the dishwashing. (My father's contribution was moving the furniture and vacuuming with the big, heavy Hoover after the guests went home.) She took great pleasure in bringing people together for happy or good causes, and she did a fine job of it. When she finally put away the last, wiped dish, she would sit down to rest and *kvell.*

A wonderful combination of head, heart, and soul, she used her manifold gifts well and left many memories for her adoring grandchildren. Most of what she set out to do, she accomplished. At age forty, when she decided to go to college, she sat (nervously, at first) in classrooms with twenty-year olds and excelled. Five years later, she began a successful career.

But she remained an old-fashioned *eshes chayil,* a pre-woman's-lib woman who would never have dreamed of using her maiden name, or of signing "Ms." Her husband's name was fine with her. In fact, it was a badge of honor. It meant she was my father's wife.

I considered myself her natural successor, and always assumed I would be just like her. But then I discovered that I didn't quite have the same style, class, aplomb. She was in a different league.

Hers was a hard act to follow, but she left a bright, clear trail for anyone who'd like to try. There are one granddaughter and several great-granddaughters, *ken yirbu,* walking around with her genes. One of them, a dark-eyed little girl, carries her name. Perhaps one day, please G-d, they will take up where she left off.

# This Isn't a Zoo!

I like animals, I really do. I'm not afraid of dogs; I'll pat cats; I make funny noises at parakeets and I have cleaned out aquariums galore.

The prohibition of *tza'ar ba'alei chayim* — causing pain to an animal — is a concept we grew up with, and as far as I'm concerned, good people are upset if they see an animal mistreated. A woman told me that on a first date, when the young man she was with kicked a cat out of the way on the sidewalk, she refused to meet him again. I understood perfectly.

Every living animal embodies the miracle of life. A piano won't produce another piano; a bicycle won't give birth to mini-bikes. This mind-boggling miracle is reserved for the kingdom of the living, and this being the case, all living things deserve to be treated with respect and care.

My mother, *z"l*, had a long, honorable history of good relations with the animal kingdom. She kept a carp in the bathtub for a week, fed a big turtle by hand one summer (we used to go fly-catching for the turtle) and she once freed a bird from the mouth of a cat. And all this after having been nipped in the back by a horse when she was just a little girl!

One glorious memory of a shared activity in the animal realm was the night my mother and I acted as midwives to our small family mutt. We were expecting a puppy or two at most, but we harvested seven tiny yelping balls of fur. My father insisted that mother and offspring be moved to the basement first thing the next morning. He was not running a maternity hospital for canines in his house if he could help it!

But all of this animal activity did not prepare me for my children's husbandry career. It's one thing to be the kid in the house who wants an animal, and another to be the mother who isn't quite so sure!

Imagine a dirty, dusty, adorable eight-year-old boy, standing in the doorway with a terribly worried expression on his face, holding a similarly dirty, dusty, adorable puppy.

"No!" I say a bit too loudly, before he can even open his mouth. "Wherever you got it from, take it back!"

"But, Imma, he has no home. This American girl came here for a year and she's leaving next week and she can't take him on the plane. She says maybe we can keep him for a week and find him a home."

"No!" I thunder. "Take him back. If she owns him, he's an American dog. I'm sure she can get him a passport."

"But, Imma, he can't go to America. He only understands Hebrew. It's only for a week. Look at him. He's so little. He can sleep with me. I'll feed him. Just for a week."

The animal in question peeped up at me from under a big floppy ear and wagged a tiny tail.

"Don't weaken or you'll never get out of it!" I tell myself. "Just remember the last time!" I do, and I shudder. The entire neighborhood camped out in our house to watch our first puppy grow, move, eat, sleep, bark. The water bill tripled from constant hand-washing. We had to designate rooms to eat, *daven*, learn, live without the puppy. A neighbor complained that the dog thought her door was a tree and she was tired of mopping up after him. Finally, Abba put down his foot. "It's me or the dog," he said, his hand on a suitcase.

There are many things we can give up in this world, but our Abba is definitely not one of them. So our search for a new puppy-home began. We didn't expect any trouble for, as everyone knows, all the world loves a puppy. Or so we thought. But we were in for a surprise. Not a soul wanted *this* puppy. Not even for free. Not even when we offered to pay them for taking him!

Eventually, we gave him to a family on a moshav after having promised our kids they could visit him at least once a week for the rest of their lives. Fortunately, after they were satisfied that the dog was happy and well, their interest petered out, and our weekly visits to the country came to an end.

But I didn't want to go through all that again, so this time, I stood my ground (feeling all the while like the Original Witch). This adorable American puppy was going to fly to the United States or be housed at a different Israeli address, not ours. My son took him back.

❈  ❈  ❈

Then there was the snake. A well-known Israeli ophiologist (ophiology, for the uninitiated, is the branch of zoology dealing with snakes) lives in our neighborhood. For a long period of time, the neighborhood boys (the girls had more sense) crawled around the fields and empty lots collecting specimens for him. The parents were blissfully unaware of this particular project until one of our kids came home with a squirmy collection of boxes and bottles.

"Pinchas isn't home. He's on vacation," he said. "These snakes are worth money. He pays us half a shekel per snake. You don't want us to throw them out, do you?"

As a matter of fact, I did. But I had not only my son to contend with, I had a contingent of ten-year-olds who offered me scores of seemingly valid reasons why nothing would happen if the snakes stayed with us for a day or two. The snakes couldn't stay in *their* homes because of scores of other seemingly valid reasons (every one Maternal).

I must have been low on vitamins that day, because I grudgingly agreed, but with conditions.

1. All snake jars must be tightly sealed.
2. Holes for oxygen in jar caps must be SMALL.
3. No boxes could be used. Any snake without a jar would have to double up with a friend.
4. All snake jars must be kept together on the porch.
5. All snakes must depart within 24 hours or else !!! (Or else what? I asked myself. I'll boil them in oil? Guillotine them? Free them in the front yard? I decided not to think about it.)

The terms were accepted and the house returned to normal the next day. Or so I thought. Until I saw something slither across the floor a week later. I'm proud to say I did not scream. But I did gag. And it took a minute or two until I caught my breath. When I did, I hit the top of the decibel scale. "WHAT IS THIS SNAKE DOING IN MY HOUSE???"

Well, it seems that Pinchas the ophiologist stayed on vacation longer than planned. My son wasn't willing to divest himself of his valuable property and there was no place else to bring the snakes, so he put the jars in a box and the box under his bed and that's all there was to it.

"You mean," I gagged again, "you mean you were sleeping with them in the room?"

"It was too cold for them outside. They aren't poisonous or

anything like that, Imma, really they aren't. They're harmless. Wanna see?"

"No!" I jumped. "How can they be harmless when they almost gave me a heart attack? And why are they crawling around the room?"

"I let them out of the jars for a few minutes every day so they can have a little exercise. I don't want them to get cramped. I guess I forgot to put one back in . . . "

We stripped the room and removed all the furniture and bedding, just to make sure nothing else was exercising, and my son took the snakes down to the shelter. It was definitely one of our creepier experiences.

❈ ❈ ❈

We had lots of goldfish (which died), and guppies (who reproduced at an astronomical rate. My mother was at the first birthing while we were out of town. She immediately called. "What am I supposed to do with them?" she asked frantically. "There were seven of them yesterday and there are thirty today!") And we also had snails.

Snails are interesting creatures. You put them in the aquarium to keep the place clean, but they reproduce by leaving grayish spots (which are actually clusters of eggs) on the sides of the aquarium. Then, one day when you aren't paying any attention, those eggs turn into little snails, and the next thing you know, the entire aquarium is a solid pack of snails who are busy laying new egg spots on top of the old ones, sort of like second and third floors. We supplied all the people on the block with free snails until they started sending snails (and their babies) back to us. It was a horror.

I tried to find out if it was halachically permissible to throw the snails into the garbage or down the toilet. I don't remember what the answer was, but to my children (and to me) it smacked of coldblooded murder, so we dismissed that idea.

We finally gave the entire aquarium — fish, pump, thermostat, lights, snails, rocks and all — to a friend as a "gift" in return for a promise not to ever bring any of it back — especially not the snails.

I did put my foot down when presented with chicks (always remember — a chick is only a baby rooster in disguise!) and hamsters (too reminiscent of mice). But the best of the lot was the kid.

(Note: While reading the following, please keep in mind that we live in an apartment building. On the third floor.)

In many places in Israel you can find Bedouins grazing flocks of goats in empty lots or fields, even in the cities. Comes the spring, and most of the mama goats have kids. I will admit, a baby goat is a charming thing. Thin, soft, nimble, shy — it just begs to be hugged.

On a trip down to Arad in the Negev, a Bedouin offered to sell us a kid. That was all my kids had to hear. "It'll grow and give us milk and we can make cheese. And it's quiet. It doesn't crow like a rooster or bark like a dog, so it won't bother anyone." So went the discussion. (I pointed out that it baa's, which can be considered noisy, but they disagreed.)

"We can spin wool, imagine!" (I couldn't.) "And it doesn't need special food. A goat will eat almost anything." (Like the bushes and trees in front of the house.) "And it's soft and brown and white with long ears and isn't it adorable?" Yes, I had to admit, it was.

For a moment, I wavered. Until I heard the Voice of Reason emanating from my husband's throat. "No goats!" it decreed, and I knew in my heart of hearts that it was not to be.

The kids (mine, not the goat's) were crushed. It took a hefty bribe of ice cream to get them smiling again. And a promise, that if and when we ever move to a farm (who? us???), *bli neder* and *b'ezras Hashem*, we'd let them have as many animals as they like.

✼ ✼ ✼

I'm hoping they'll all be grown up by then and won't want any. Of course, someday, if their children want a puppy or two (or a mule or a goat) I won't mind one bit. In fact, I think it would be a splendid idea. Pets are such a wonderful experience — for other people's children.

# Timeless Teachers

ost people can remember one special teacher — the one who cared, who really taught, the one who made a difference. I remember one too.

It was in the days when day schools weren't what they are now. It was a different era when, except for certain schools in New York, boys and girls learned together (otherwise there would have been five kids in a class instead of ten); when teachers were Yiddish-speaking refugees from Europe; when school was dismissed several times a winter as the boiler broke down with increasing frequency; in short, when day schools were not exactly what you'd call mainstream. Only children of highly dedicated Jewish parents (on the one side), or children who were problematic and were therefore unwelcome in public schools (the other side) graced the portals of Jewish schools.

They were a no-frills affair, these pioneer day schools: no swimming, no gym, no laboratories, no libraries, no home economics or mechanics, or school trips; nothing except classroom learning, seven-and-one-half hours per day plus one-half hour for lunch — when there was time. In this no-nonsense atmosphere, the quality of your learning experience was absolutely and solely dependent upon one factor — your teacher.

For several years of my young life, I was lucky. Every morning, a wonderful, stoutish man with a wispy white beard energetically pumped me and the rest of my restless classmates full of the glory of G-d's Torah, the knowledge of His heritage, the uniqueness of His people. His name was Rabbi Eliyahu Bloch, and he showered us, the new generation of "Amerikanishers," with love and devotion. He prepared his lessons — the holy wisdom of the Torah — as carefully as though we were a *Yoreh Deah shiur,* and spiced them all with common sense and lots of pedagogical creativity. It made no difference that we were only fifth graders. He taught us with a fiery passion.

He couldn't have been old, although to my young eyes, he always seemed elderly. I thought he was tall, but in later years I realized that he was on the short side. I never thought to ask where he had come from, although I assume it was somewhere in Lithuania. He was an independent, disconnected entity in my existence — not really part of my normal, everyday life, yet a deep, intrinsic part of the warm Jewish world I lived in. And he filled this world with knowledge.

Today, many years later, I still find it difficult to believe how much we learned and how far we traveled as we sat there at our scratched-up desks (which were so old they had inkwells!), squinting at an old-fashioned glaring, black blackboard (the school couldn't afford the newer, green, glare-free boards until a later date), and listening to a heavily accented, highly unconventional English. But learn we did — *Chumash,*

*Navi, dinim; Ivris* and Yiddish (including — penmanship — in both languages because it was "important to write legibly"); prayers, history and all sorts of vital things which refuse to be classified.

*Rashi* was a force to be reckoned with: we could never begin to read him until we had first figured out "what *Rashi* was asking." (I tried that with my own kids years later only to be told that it was irrelevant; the main thing was to get on with it. I wonder if their teacher knew "what *Rashi* was asking"!)

*Davening* was serious business. No mumbling allowed; words were to be said clearly and correctly. Including *sheva na's* and *sheva nach's*. Each and every one. I left Rabbi Bloch's class knowing most of *Shacharis* by heart. I could even write it all out. Correctly. (No mean feat for a twelve-year-old American girl!) And even today, his two "*davening* signs" are clearly engraved on my mind: *Da lifnei mi ata omeid* — know before Whom you stand — and *Shivisi Hashem l'negdi tamid* — I shall place G-d before me forever.

We sang, too. In the days before Mordechai Ben David and Avraham Fried. Dozens of songs. Songs for the prayers and songs for the holidays and songs for *Shabbos* and songs for learning Hebrew. I can see him now, holding his high, black silk yarmulke and pointing to the words on the shiny blackboard with his wooden pointer. (The boys in class would, on rare occasions, feel this pointer on their hands as a reminder of better behavior. Girls were only reprimanded verbally.)

When I came home singing the *trop* one day, my father questioned the wisdom of teaching "boys' topics" to girls. (Since our small class consisted of both boys and girls, we learned whatever they learned.) Yet that knowledge has been a constant help in reading the *Chumash* properly, and has given me great pleasure through years of listening to *krias haTorah*. Rabbi Bloch knew that no knowledge is ever wasted.

And, I must add, in those pre-feminist days, Rabbi Bloch never for a moment transmitted the feeling that "boys' learning" was more important than girls'. There was never a question that Jewish girls were absolutely, unquestionably vital to the welfare of the nation and that they must be learned. Perhaps this fierce feeling of pride which he instilled in us is one reason that so many of the feminist questions women ponder today do not seem particularly pertinent to me and my friends.

Even more important than the book learning were the things Rabbi Bloch discussed: How he refused to change his proper, given, Jewish name when he arrived at Ellis Island, for instance. I could just see him — a real greenhorn, barely speaking English, with no family to support him, arguing with the immigration official who wanted to turn him into "Eli Block."

"I am the only Bloch listed in the Chicago phone directory," he told us. "And the only Eliyahu." He was, too.

Yom Kippur nights he stayed awake and learned in the small shul where he *davened* on Chicago's South Side. I remember thinking how hard that must be (no one stayed after the *davening* in our shul!). But he made it sound not like a hardship, but a privilege, an act of love and devotion. And in my mind's eye, I had this image of Rabbi Bloch as a sort of earthly angel, wrapped in his white *tallis* and sitting in shul with the *sifrey Torah*, pleading with *Hakadosh Baruch Hu* for the welfare of *Klal Yisrael*. Perhaps in this case, a child's image and the truth were not so far apart.

Lastly, I remember his burning, unending, overwhelming love for the Land of Israel. He himself had never actually seen this Land — at least not with his eyes. He had seen it, however, through the eyes of the Torah, and like the Torah, he made it glow, live, beckon.

I remember the day he told us that Jews were fighting for their lives in *Eretz Yisrael* and things were not going well. It was in the midst of Israel's War for Independence in 1948. He explained how the Jews of Shushan had been saved by the prayers of the children. Now, he said, the *rabbanim* had declared a day of prayer and it was our turn and our duty to stand up and pray with all our heart and all our might for our brothers in *Eretz Yisrael.* Surely *Hashem* would listen to us — young children, born of a long and bitter exile — and would bring victory to the Jewish army.

I have said *Avinu Malkeynu* many times since that fifth-grade class, but I doubt if any time has matched the fervor and *kavanah* of that teary prayer. I like to think that in G-d's great scheme of things, the *davening* in our class helped.

Although Rabbi Bloch had two sons, he once told us that we, his students, were his real children. I heard the great sadness in his voice and I understood that somehow, in the great melting pot that was America, his sons had gone a different way. For many years, this distressed me. But with the birth of the *teshuvah* movement, I found comfort. Surely, their *zechus avos* would bring his grand or great-grandchildren back to the lifeline of his people.

I think Rabbi Bloch would be proud and happy — and amazed beyond words! — if he could see his former students today. They include an impressive number of *rabbanim, roshei yeshivah, rebbetzins,* teachers and wonderful *"amcha"* both in America and in Israel. And many of us are still good friends.

On second thought, perhaps he wouldn't be amazed at all. There was never any doubt in his mind that the tree of Torah would take root again, even in America. And that his "children" would be the branches and the flowers and the leaves.

# A Red-headed Lesson in Love

 don't remember what she looked like, except that she was old, short, and had an ill-fitting, bright red wig on her head. But I remember her nonetheless. It's such a little, funny kind of story that you'd think it's not even worth mentioning, but it has remained in my mind for nearly forty years. If something stays with you that long, it must mean something.

It happened on a Friday night in our old shul on Chicago's West Side. There were rarely enough men to fill the big, upstairs shul on Friday nights, so the *minyan* met downstairs in the smaller *beis medrash*.

When a friend and I decided to start coming for *Kabbalas Shabbos*, we were not only the youngest females in the women's section, we were also the only females under the age of sixty-five or seventy. But I enjoyed the cozy *minyan*, the dim lights, the sounds of *davening,* and even the smells of the place (a mixture of leather, old books, and wood combined with the particular soap used to clean the floors.).

The presence of two young girls was a cause for great excitement among the older women who scrutinized our clothing, checked to see if we could really read Hebrew and keep up with the prayers, and, in general, discussed us shamelessly and to our faces. If we didn't show up one week, we had to explain (in Yiddish) why we hadn't come. Then the explanation would be passed back, row by row, until everyone was properly apprised of the change in our schedule.

Sometimes it seemed to me that our appearance must have touched a sensitive spot in the hearts of those women. Where were their many children and grandchildren? Chances are that most of them were not praying on Friday nights. Theirs was the American Melting Pot generation, anxiously climbing the ladder to success. It was a generation of good Jewish "hearts," but very little Jewish knowledge or practice. And so we found ourselves "adopted" and, like all children every-where, answerable to our elders for our deeds.

I thought it was rather touching and didn't mind being the center of so much elderly attention. One woman in particular took us under her wing. She was a rather quiet, wrinkled, unpretentious, little lady with a large, bright red wig, utterly inappropriate to her size and age. She kept an eye, not so much on us (we didn't need it) but on the other women, just to make sure they didn't overly attend to our needs.

One hot, summery *Shabbos* eve, we showed up as usual. Or more or less as usual. We came wearing sandals. Without stockings. In those days, stockings, especially in the summer, were not part of the normal dress code among young religious girls in the Midwest. (Probably not in the Mideast either.) The minute we entered the shul, ten pairs of elderly eyes went straight down to our feet and ten pairs of elderly lips began to "tsk, tsk, tsk."

"*Ohn heisen? Vi geyt men zu shul ohn heisen?*" they asked, shaking their heads disapprovingly. ("Without stockings? How can you come to shul without stockings?")

Now I must admit that I had never heard, nor had it ever occurred to me, that one could not go to shul (or anywhere else for that matter) without stockings. In Chicago's hot, sticky summer, our socks (we were still too young for stockings) were left behind as a matter of course along with our sweaters, gloves, boots and heavy underwear! I thought that the idea of wearing socks as a further embellishment of dressy *Shabbos* clothes was unusual, but my friend was annoyed. Comes our Little Old Lady with the Red Sheitel to the rescue!

"For shame! Leave them alone! Some youngsters finally come to shul and you chase them away because of stockings? Old women with stockinged feet and empty heads, that's what you are! Where are your grandchildren? They wear stockings? I should live to see it! G-d cannot hear children who pray without stockings? Do they pray with their feet? Moshe Rabbeinu prayed without shoes!"

She waved them away and stood guard over us, holding herself five-feet-and-one-inch high, bristling like a lightning rod. (She could only stand over us because we were sitting; if we stood up, we towered over her.) But despite her lack of height, no knight in shining armor could have done better. Our well-meaning advisers shuffled back to their seats and hid shamefacedly behind their prayer books.

Eventually, our Friday evening appearances petered out. But I remember my lady. Her kindly, wrinkled smile, her wise heart, and her loving concern had left their mark on a young girl's soul.

Today, whenever I find myself thinking or sounding too judgmental, I see her still, shaking her bright red wig and her small, crooked finger at all the guardians of things holy. I know that she must be at it still, keeping an eye on the *ezras nashim* in some heavenly shul, making sure that all comers are made welcome, and that all prayers are allowed to reach their destination.

Such is the power of love.

# Glossary

ABI GEZUNT   As long as we're healthy!; G-d bless you!
ALIYAH   immigrating to Israel
ALIYAH, ALIYOS   call to recite the blessing on the Torah
AM YISRAEL   the Jewish people
AMCHA   laymen
AMORAIM   Sages of the Gemara
ARONEI-KODESH   Torah arks
ASSUR   forbidden
AVEILUS   mourning
AVRAHAM AVINU   Our father Abraham
AVRAHAM HAIVRI   Abraham the Hebrew
B'EZRAS HASHEM   with G-d's help; please G-d
B'SAMIM   spices (used during Havdalah at the end of Sabbath)
B'SHA'AH TOVA   at an auspicious time
BAAL TASHCHIS   a wasteful sin
BALABATIM   laymen
BALEBATESHA   proper
BARUCH HASHEM   Thank G-d
BAYIS   home, house
BEIS HAMIKDASH   the Holy Temple in Jerusalem
BEIS MIDRASH   house of learning
BEN (BNEI) TORAH   carefully observant Jew(s)
BIMAH   center platform
BITACHON   faith; trust
BIZ AH HUHNDRED UN TZVANZIG   (May you live) to 120!
BLI NEDER   without intending to take an oath
BRACHAH, BRACHOS   blessing(s)
BUBBY   grandmother
CHAG   holiday
CHALAV YISRAEL   milk produced under kashruth supervision
CHAMETZ   leaven
CHAMSIN   Middle East heat wave, originating in the desert
CHAS V'CHALILAH   G-d forbid
CHASSIDISHE   pertaining to the chassidic culture or community

CHAZAL   our Sages, may their memories be for a blessing
CHAZZAN, CHAZZANIM   cantor(s)
CHEIN   grace, charm
CHESSED   lovingkindness
CHEYN   grace, charm
CHINUCH   education
CHOL HAMOED   the intermediate days of Passover and Sukkos
CHEVRON   Hebron
CHOLEH   sick person
CHUMASH   the Five Books of Moses
CHUPPAH   the marriage canopy
CHUTZ LA'ARETZ   a term for anyplace outside the Land of Israel
DAVEN   pray
DAVID HAMELECH   King David
DINIM   laws
EMUNAH   faith
ERETZ YISRAEL   the Land of Israel
EREV   eve
ESHES CHAYIL   a woman of valour; a genuine wife and mother
EZER   a help, an aid
EZRAS NASHIM   the women's section in the synagogue
FLEISHIG   foodstuffs containing meat
FRUM   religious, observant
GAN EDEN   the Garden of Eden
GEMARA   the Talmud
GOLDENEH MEDINEH   the country of gold (the United States)
GLATT   meat kosher according to special halachic standards
GOLUS   diaspora
GOYIM   gentiles
HACHNASAS ORCHIM   hospitality
HAKADOSH BARUCH HU   the Holy One, Blessed is He; G-d
HALACHAH   Jewish religious law
HASHEM   G-d
HECHSHER   rabbinical certification
HESDER   an arrangement for young men in Israel to both learn in a
    yeshiva and serve in the army
IVRIS, IVRIT   Hebrew
KABBALAS SHABBOS   the Sabbath Eve prayers
KRIAS HATORAH   the reading of the Torah
KALLAH   a bride
KAVANAH   concentration
KEDUSHAH   holiness

KEN YIRBU   May it (they) multiply!

KEVER   grave

KEVER RACHEL   Rachel's Tomb in Bethlehem

KIDDUSH   sanctification of the Sabbath over a cup of wine; also, a collation at which Kiddush is recited

KIPPA, KIPPOT   skullcap(s)

KLAL YISRAEL   the community of Israel

KOLLEL   yeshivah for married students

KOTEL   the Western Wall of the Temple in Jerusalem

KRIAS SHEMA   see Shema

KVELL   to tingle with satisfaction

LASHON HAKODESH   the holy tongue (Hebrew)

LASHON HARA   gossip; slander

LECHAYIM   a toast, "to life"

LEHAVDIL   to differentiate

LIMUDEI KODESH   sacred learning

MACHZOR   holiday prayer book

MAKOLET   grocery store

MALITZ YOSHER   an advocate

MAMA LOSHEN   mother tongue

MASHIACH   the Messiah

ME'ARAT HAMACHPEYLA   Tomb of the Patriarchs in Hebron

MEHUDAR   special

MENTSH, MENTSHEN   decent human being(s)

MESHUGASIM   eccentricities

MESHULACHIM   fundraisers; emissaries

MEZUZAH, MEZUZOS   handwritten parchment Shema scrolls placed on doorposts of Jewish homes

MIKVEH   ritual bath

MILCHIG   foodstuffs containing dairy ingredients

MINHAGIM   customs

MINIM   kinds, species

MINYAN   quorum of ten men for prayer

MITZVAH, MITZVOS   a commandment, commandments

MODEH ANI   the first prayer said upon arising

MOSHE RABBEINU   Our teacher Moses

MUKTZEH   forbidden to be moved on the Sabbath and holidays

NACHAS   satisfaction

NAVI, NEVIIM   prophet(s)

NESHAMAH   soul

NIGGUN, NIGGUNIM   melody, melodies

PAREVE   foodstuffs containing neither dairy nor meat products

PASUL   invalid
PECKLACH   small packages
PESACH   Passover
PESACHDIK   fitting for Passover
PUSHKE   charity box
RABBANIM   rabbis
RAMBAM   Maimonides
REBBE   rabbi, teacher
REBBETZIN   rabbi's wife
ROSH YESHIVAH, ROSHEI YESHIVAH   head(s) of the yeshivah
SEDARIM   ritual meal on first two nights of Passover
SEFER, SEFARIM   book, books (especially sacred books)
SEUDAH   meal
SHABBOS   the Sabbath
SHABBOSDIK   fitting for the Sabbath
SHACHARIS   the morning prayer
SHALACH MANOS   Purim gifts of food
SHATNEZ   the biblical prohibition to wear linen and wool woven
   into one garment
SHECHEM   Nablus
SHEITEL   a wig; worn as a head covering by Jewish women
SHEMA   declaration of a Jew's belief in G-d's Oneness
SHEMITAH   the Sabbatical agricultural year in Israel
SHEP NACHAS   to have satisfaction
SHEVA NA   mobile schwa (a vowel point)
SHEVA NACH   quiescent schwa (a vowel point)
SHIDDUCH   a match
SHLEP   drag, carry
SHTEIBEL   a Chassidic synagogue
SHTREIMEL   fur hat worn by some men on the Sabbath and
   holidays
SHUL   synagogue
SIDDUR   a prayer book
SIFREI KODESH   sacred books
SIFREY TORAH   Torah scrolls
SIMCHAH   joy; a celebration
SIN'AS ESAV   the hatred of Esau for Jacob; anti-Semitism
SINA'AS CHINAM   causeless hatred
SPODIK   a form of shtreimel
SUKKAH   temporary dwelling used during Succos holiday
TAHOR   pure; ritually clean
TALLIS   prayer shawl

TALMIDEI CHACHAMIM   Torah scholars
TANAIM   Sages of the Mishnah
TASHLICH   prayer said near a body of water on Rosh Hashanah
TEFILLAH   prayer; a prayer
TEFILLAS HADERECH   the Traveler's Prayer
TEFILLIN   phylacteries
TEICH   to translate line by line
TESHUVAH   return to Jewish observance
TIYUL   a hike, outing
TROP   cantillation for Torah reading
TZEDAKAH   charity
TZITZIS   tallis fringes
TZNIUS   modesty
YARMULKE   skullcap
YERICHO   Jericho
YESHIVA   a talmudical academy
YETZER HARA   the evil inclination
YISHUV   community, settlement
YISURIM   suffering
YOM TOV   a holiday
YOTZEI   to fulfill one's obligations
Z"L   May his (her, their) memory be for a blessing!
ZECHUS AVOS   merit of the forefathers
ZECHUYOS   merits
ZEIDY   grandfather
ZEMIROS   the songs sung at the Sabbath table